PREFACE

For some considerable time it has been apparent that all is not well with Information Systems development. This is related to several factors, including:

❏ How individual companies and organisations express and design their Information Systems.

❏ The influence the user has over that development.

❏ The rquirement for more flexible approaches to Information Systems development.

Most organisations have a set of information systems that are used to provide: overall control and short term management; medium term control and direction; long term control and decision making. The development, use and maintenance of these may be triggered by both external and internal factors. By using a flexible approach to the analysis and design of systems we should be able to improve our confidence in the final product.

The major problem is one of choosing the correct methodology for our development. If we turn the question on its head and determine what factors we are looking for – by asking precisely what we wish to express – we may be able to build a 'Tool set' which is applicable to most Information Systems development projects.

The book is an attempt to set down a framework for a user-centred approach to the development of IS projects. The first part concentrates on exactly what we are trying to express, and why. It then moves on to sketch briefly the operation of two contrasting standard system design methodologies. Chapter four discusses the environment needed for automated systems design and development work and proposes a platform for these automated tools.

The second part of the book deals with design and implementation considerations, as well as a brief introduction to the management of projects. It discusses the man machine interface, software quality and the data store which are all of importance in the design of systems.

As users become more sophisticated, they requires systems to be more presentable, user-friendly and adaptable to changing circumstances. They also require them to be more reliable, and to be proved to be more reliable. Therefore, the last part in this section deals with the management and estimation of costs, which are closely related to specification and delivery. Some guidelines are provided on how to estimate costings for software projects.

The third and last part of the book is a case study. This provides practice in the skills that students of systems analysis and design need to acquire. It provides a framework for both discussion and practical development.

Stuart Wattam

Contents

1

Introduction to Software Engineering

Objectives

Define a System in the context of data processing.

Identify the constituent parts of a system.

Describe the System Life Cycle, and what it affects.

Identify what is wrong with current development methods.

Describe software development in the context of software engineering.

What is a System?

Perhaps the best place to start is with a general definition of a *System:*

'A System is an organised collection of constituent parts, such that it displays a purpose that is implicit in the organisation of those constituent parts.'

Most large organisations which adopt some form of computerisation for their procedures or, indeed, those that do not, have inside the operation identifiable systems under the definition above. As stated, the organisation's systems need not be computer based, but they do, however, share some common characteristics as systems. There are three subclassifications of systems that can be roughly categorised into Technical, Institutional and Organisational. Furthermore, within these categorisations there is a further classification of Hard/Soft or Open/Closed system types (see Figure 1.1). Further classifications can be made, and the definition of a system given above is not sufficient for our needs [1].

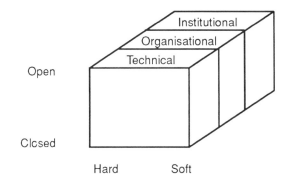

Figure 1.1 The broad classification of systems viewed as sections in the domain of all systems that exist within an organisation

Organisational

The level of operations that are in direct contact with a specific operation are normally classified as organisational systems, whether these systems are at board level or on the shop floor. The common factor is the supervisory nature of the systems, i.e. the provision of information in a manner which enables a supervisory strategy to be enacted on the organisation.

Normally there is also an allowance for some form of human management and fine tuning to take place, even if this is only analysis of output from the system.

Institutional

These types of system have usually been developed to meet legal or mandatory requirements, and take the form of systems which safeguard the organisation's practices and procedures.

Secondly, they also provide the 'day-to-day' performance of functions which are needed to make the organisation work.

Technical

Here the systems are mainly concerned with supportive tasks; development, production co-ordination, engineering and scientific work. They can be readily identified since they need a specialist to implement them; a communications system is a good example.

The category in which the individual system belongs is more problematic. It is rare to find a system that has all the characteristics of one, but none of any of the others. Furthermore, this is complicated by consideration as to whether the system is Open/Closed or Hard/Soft.

Open or Closed

The main characteristic of an open system is that it continuously adapts itself to outside influences, so that its responses are not always the same (e.g. a biological system). A physical system, such as a speed governor on an engine, can be looked upon as a closed system since it obeys fixed, deterministic rules.

Hard or Soft

The contrast is based on how well the system under consideration is understood. If the objectives are known and well stated, and the constraints readily identified, then the system is 'hard'.

Therefore, most systems in any organisation will display the characteristics of all or some of the defined types of system. There is one distinct fact that has been left out of these considerations: the use of computers has led to the adoption of a 'hard system' approach since this type is more readily definable and analysable, and produces good results in the form of a requirement analysis. Also, when a comparison is made against the system it replaced, a good match is found.

However, the systems we are mainly concerned with in software engineering have up to now been well defined and fairly easy to analyse. Although this is changing, the constituent parts of any computer system are easily identifiable, and can be split for convenience.

From the view of the computer system these constituent parts take the form of hardware, software and 'liveware' (the people that are going to use it!). These components are organised into a logical set of functions intended to perform a task or group of tasks (production of the company accounts, for example). The logical processes are such that they can be written down in a finite number of steps, and performed in sequence. The expression of these processes is a set of serial rules which are translated into the software for the machine to follow, or into a series of user interactions which are required to guide the software. Therefore, the set of rules is an extension of the software into the user's environment, and his/her control over the operation is fundamentally affected by how the computer system interfaces with the user.

The constituents of the embryonic computer system have traditionally been the result of the study or analysis of the existing system, be it manual or computer based. This analysis results in some form of specification to which the software is written. This whole process is tied to the idea that all problems can be expressed in an inflexible and concrete form, so that the resulting computer system is 'produced' in much the same way as a car is produced, from raw materials in a finite number of steps.

The constituent parts of a system are so diverse that the production of software is a complex task. The result of any work a computer department may perform ranges from the implementation of a general purpose 'off-the-shelf' package through to a 'bespoke' system written in a high-level-language. This may result in a mismatch between what the user wants and what is provided. Normally a considerable length of time passes, during which the user's initial requirements may well change, from first idea to final implementation.

It is the interaction with the user, and his/her requirementsthat have been the cause of a lot of problems in software engineering. It has also led to the re-evaluation of software development, and the methods by which that development is performed.The importance of software in systems engineering is fundamental to the adoption of a method of design that gives us the desired end product, i.e. the method must evolve to accommodate changes in both user perspectives and the equipment on which we use our systems. Also it must take into account any changes in theoretical work or the adoption of working standards and practice.

Software sophistication has to some extent lagged behind the improvement of hardware. The reason for this is that the needs and goals of the users are different from those of the people who develop the software. Consider the progress made in data processing over the short period of time we have been performing this task. At the very early stage the programs that ran on the machines were very limited in what they were intended to achieve, and were written with specific goals and objectives, by the people that would use them. At the advent of larger more powerful machines, software was written for a more general clientele, e.g. a generic application such as stock control, purchase ledger, and payroll. The third phase was integration of these control systems into linked software such as accounting systems, manufacturing control systems and general management information systems coupled with databases, communications and micros. The decentralisation of power?

Users now have micros on their desks that will run some very sophisticated software and they expect the same standard on whatever machine the application may be running. This implies decentralisation not only in processing power but in support, advice and expertise. Resources are moving from the traditional central data processing department to user departments, all with different requirements, goals, and hopefully satisfactory software systems. The software that runs in this environment has to go through a rigorous process of adaptation and transformation in power and applicability, so as to assist the user in the business task.

The application package, or piece of software, is written to perform a given task. It is assumed that the task is associated with the organisational requirements and a system type identified earlier. What factors can we identify that are common to all?

There is the user interface of control of processing and communication for input and results; the processing requirements which transform the input data to the output data; and the storage of results, information and data. The two important factors which should govern our design of software are the user interface and the storage of information. Recently there has been a development in the interest shown in Artificial Intelligence (AI) techniques, and the applicability of these to business tasks. There has also been pressure to develop 'Open Systems' so that users are not locked into vendor-dependent software which have different interfaces. Witness the use of menu selection (pull-down, pop-up, on-line, help and so on), and common control keys that perform system tasks, e.g. F1 will usually get you help on micro software. Hence the move by corporates to standardise on hardware and software in the organisation.

These stages of development in the use of computing can be witnessed in most organisations. Some areas will be well advanced while others will not. The systems in operation will therefore be influenced by the sophistication and expectations of the user.

The System Life Cycle

The basis for the analysis of systems, their interaction and dependencies on resource usage can be attempted by use of the traditional Rayleigh curve, which identifies the effort versus the time spent on a typical software project. Figure 1.2 shows this effect. There are numerous papers and books on how closely this curve is obeyed [2].

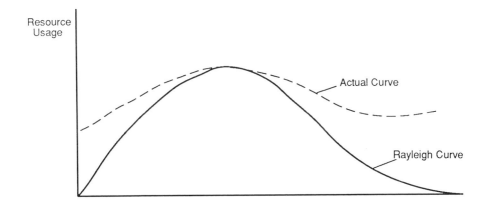

Figure 1.2 The life cycle of a system approximated to the Rayleigh curve for the purpose of estimating the developmental time for the project

However, from the point of view that it is a suitable vehicle on which to found a discussion of the topic, it is unsurpassed. Chapter 2 discusses the task of software estimation and costing with particular reference to the Rayleigh curve and the system life cycle.

The shape of the curve can be directly related to the resource requirements: as a software project gets under way more and more manpower is attached to it, with numbers reaching a peak and thereafter declining. However, two points can be made immediately:

❑ The curve should start at a finite value. (People start the project off!)

❑ The curve does not fall to zero. (There is always a need for maintenance or enhancements).

The effect of these modifications is shown again in Figure 1.2. The tail of the curve extends further out, and is higher than one might expect in a 'normal' Rayleigh curve. Indeed, the smooth curve will become stepped and disjointed.

The actual life cycle is considerably more complex than that identified above. There are certain functions that have to be included. Figure 1.3, opposite, identifies the other characteristics of the system life cycle.

Systems Definition/Requirements

The traditional approach has been an identification of user requirements, and an analysis of possible inputs, outputs, machines and software. This usually takes the form of a short report, which is carried forward for consideration or adoption for further development, and may include:

Functional Design and Specification

A more detailed design of what is required of the system, breaking it down into procedures, detailed inputs and outputs and data storage requirements, personnel requirements, costs/benefits and a project plan.

Development of the System

Detailed design of input, output, files and procedures along with production and testing of the procedures as they are written, in the high-level language or the development package chosen.

Maintenance and Operation

The use of the system, its upkeep and running, either by the specialist or the end user of the system, notes of errors and their correction.

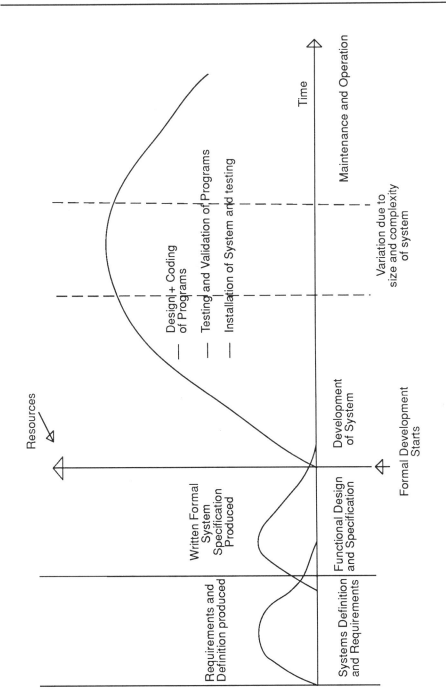

Figure 1.3 System Life Cycle viewed as a serial process

I have split the cycle into distinct phases for convenience of definition: there are other divisions that can be made, and are made. There are also other phases of the development cycle within those specified. The whole area has been well trodden before, and numerous books teach the methods of 'systems analysis' by going through the phases one by one, and giving check lists of documents that are to be produced at each stage, and the activities that the analyst must perform at each of the relevant stages of the project. The actual production of the program has also been the subject of many books [3,4,5].

These two main areas of analysis and programming have produced a wide variety of methodologies which are aimed at giving the would-be developer a set of tools by which he or she may develop the solution to a problem. These should also enable the exercise of some form of control over the development. By use of these methods the aim has been to increase the confidence the end user has in the product. Some of these tools and methodologies are identified in subsequent chapters.

However, what is supposed to happen as the life cycle progresses is an improvement in the knowledge of what the initial requirements are, and the functionality necessary to achieve those requirements. Thus as the start of the detailed design stage is approached, our knowledge of the system has improved, and uncertainty should be reduced as the design progresses. This is based on the way that the functional design is carried out, since at its end there should be a general idea of the various major functions that are required of the system, and how these functions are going to meet the requirements, presented in such a way that a program or series of programs can be developed from it. Otherwise the exercise produces a document which acts as a specification for pre-written software to be measured against it for conformity with requirements.

While undergoing the design process the system will have been split into manageable proportions or sections, based loosely on the programs or suites of programs that go to make up the functional areas, e.g. stock control. Within any area there are several sub-functions that need to be performed. The idea is to match if possible the action of the subfunctions to programs in the computer system.

As an example, consider a company that performs in-house and company-based training. It requires a computer system that keeps a diary of such courses. The system definition may be as follows:

The system must keep diary appointments for members of the training staff, who give seminars and training. The events must be identifiable and must be allocated a time slot and staff member, as well as subject area, level and numbers of trainees. It must also integrate with the diary of appointments.

The functional specification that one might come up with could be along the the following lines:

❑ Input of training events

❑ Amendment of training events

❑ Deletion of training events

❑ Review of diary contents.

Can we now go ahead and design this simple system? Assume that we have done a similar job before, then we could probably make educated guesses as to inputs, outputs, field lengths and files. What happens if the end user wishes to print out all courses given by a particular person in the last year, or the coming monthly loading on the large conference room? (The company has built an extension since you last saw them, a large conference room where seminars and presentations are given). Does this indicate that a redesign is required? These are some of the questions that are thrown up by the simple example given: you can probably think of many more.

Although the system identified above is fairly trivial, it does identify the differences between the steps that we follow when developing a system as in the description of the system life cycle, and the development of the system in the real world. The result is that the project slips and a lot of resources are spent on correcting omissions and mistakes made at an earlier stage, and this is one of the reasons why there seems to be a lot of effort required in the latter half of the life cycle, during maintenance and running.

We can actually identify the expenditure of effort during the life cycle of a typical commercial project [6,7,8]. Table 1.1 shows this breakdown.

Table 1.1 Expenditure of effort

Proportion	Task
1/12 th	Programming
1/6th	Systems design and analysis
1/4	System testing and implementation
1/2	Maintenance
Not included	Overheads

The maintenance figure has been put higher by some sources [1]. These figures are interesting in that even if we improve the design, analysis and production of programs and systems, there is still a requirement for subsequent testing and maintenance. The claim usually made by proponents of structured methods of analysis and programming is that they reduce the need for excessive maintenance and testing, thus improving confidence in the product.

Other types of Life Cycle

There are other types of life cycle models which we can use as the basis for development. These vary from the linear approach as above to the looser models based on overall methodologies. They consist essentially of the same stages of development, but we can identify factors within these stages that occur together at the same time. Also there is normally some form of iteration between several stages of the development cycle, therefore other life cycle models have been proposed which reflect the more dynamic nature of the development process.

The 'prototyping' model is used later to describe a method of development which takes on board a more flexible user-centred approach to development. Other life cycle models can be used such as the 'spiral' model, the 'V' model and the '4GL' development cycle, all of which may be of valid use in a development. The use of a particular model gives us a perspective, within reason, of what we should be doing and when we should be doing it.

One of the faults of current methods is that they stick rigidly to a particular model by which they attempt to control the development process. Secondly, instead of being used as an aid, they are used to manage a project and enforce production rules. Rather than being used as 'guides' and 'assistants' to the software developers, they have become a tool of management: the development manager can control the staff working on a particular project or projects instead of being used as an aid to assist project teams in meeting user requirements. The focus has been on control of the project rather than user requirements. What we need to do is satisfy both by selecting a method which gives us the necessary tools both to control projects and meet user requirements. Hopefully by following a systems engineering method we will achieve this aim.

What is Wrong with Current Development Methods?

We have a wide variety of methods, and the life cycle curve is well-known, so what is going wrong? The computer press is full of articles on 'The Applications Backlog', 'The Maintenance Crisis', 'Skills Shortages', and other related topics.

The analysis and programming tools were developed in an environment that was highly centralised. The machine and the DP (Data Processing) professionals were at a central site, often remote from the users. Also, there is a large commitment, in terms of costs for the organisation which has such a site. (Salaries of the development and support staff, as well as machine costs). Therefore it should be no surprise that this has led to development methods which do not offer sufficient flexibility, since one of the requirements for management was the increase in control over the projects offered by the tools and methodologies. Hence the adoption of the production environment, which is different from a more flexible decentralised development environment.

The application backlog appears as a result of development teams spending the time allocated to development on maintenance and upgrading of existing systems. This in turn leads to a maintenance crisis, whereby systems that are coming live were designed in the past, and hence were designed for past requirements. Modifications, sometimes called enhancements, therefore need to be added at a late stage in the development process. Systems were probably designed in such a way that end users were not considered at all. In fact they may have been the last people to be consulted!

The modern user has probably been brought up to use sophisticated systems, or has seen television programmes that show them what is possible. Therefore the expectations from any system that is delivered have increased.

To achieve what the user wants is a skilled job; but there is still a shortage of skilled computer staff!

Another factor which has added to this crisis is the falling cost of hardware. This fall has been dramatic over the years, and it is now feasible for an organisation to have a personal computer in every office, if not on every desk, and to have many machines scattered about a site or many sites, rather than a central mainframe. The result is more problems, including lack of standardisation of hardware and software, and the decentralisation of control as well as development. This leads to a conflict between existing methods for the centralised production of software to a fixed standard on a fixed machine, and the user who wishes to have more control, and a quicker response on a decentralised set of machines. If a typical commercial project is 18 to 24 months in gestation, and due to the applications backlog this slips to around 48 months, it is not surprising that the requirements will alter during this time.

Often the delivered system is unreliable, its accuracy questionable and the functions offered are variants of the ones planned in the early stages. The end result is that the user is frustrated or loses interest in the project. The cost of not getting it right is quite high, and the place where the errors or omissions occurred is significant. The cost in resources of correcting these errors or omissions in the final stages of the project is shown in Figure 1.4.

Despite the advent of structured methods, (which not all development teams use) the major resource cost is the result of errors or omissions in the analysis phase of the project. Hence the three problems exacerbate each other, compounding the difficulties of an already complex task. The solution lies in the use of automated analysis environments, structured programming methods and closer consultation with the end user..

Let us examine the causes of the software crisis more closely.

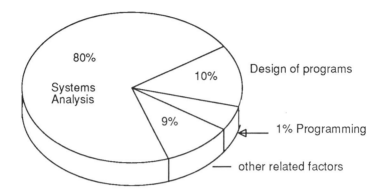

Figure 1.4 Costs of correcting errors in a typical system based on where those errors are made

Software and its Increasing Cost

The use of computer software and hardware in business has grown considerably over the last decade despite the downturn of almost every other economic indicator. The figures for the UK and US spending on the computer business are impressive. Even if we have a spending of 1% G.N.P. on automatic data processing and software, the figures are approximately £2.5 billion and £1 billion respectively. Around 50% of each is software and the proportion of software to hardware costs increases steadily. Software costs increase because of the following reasons:

❏ Each application will need the generation of new programs;

❏ Purchasing of new equipment means that existing software will either have to be modified or re-written;

❏ Programming is labour intensive and therefore strongly affected by inflation despite new techniques.

The current measure of programmer productivity is around 15 tested lines of code per day. Therefore the cost of producing software is going to be a significant portion of the total spent on any project. If the average salary is around £20,000 with overheads then a simple sum will illustrate the costs involved:

$$\frac{£2,000}{365} = £54.79 \text{ and } \frac{£54.79}{15} = £3.65 \text{ per line}$$

This sum does not take into account weekends, holidays, meetings and other unproductive activities. The eventual figure may well be double, so if your intended application is going to be several thousand lines long then a lot of money is going to be spent on it.

Software Errors and Their Impact

The later an error is detected in a software project the tougher it is to correct. In the majority of current systems the cost of testing and maintenance is around 40% of the total spent. Some would go as far as to say it is 60%. In any case it is a significant portion of the software budget. Indeed in certain cases DP departments are so tied up with maintenance of current systems that no development can take place. The increasing costs of error correction can be identified with the following components:

❏ The increase in software complexity increases the testing complexity and the amount of testing that has to be done;

❏ Notification and communication of errors become widespread and more costly and there are frequent changes in documentation;

❏ Repeating tests that have been done before is costly. It should be possible to test the portions of code that are changed but often this is not the case;

❏ The project team will have been disbanded due to leavers and other commitments.

❏ Inadequate or inaccurate requirements and needs used throughout the project due to lack of user involvement and consultation in the early stages of a development;

❏ The cost of maintaining a system is often underestimated at the outset of a project.

Software Development via an Engineering Ethos

In developing software several factors should be considered as the main ones in the development ethos. Coupled to these are other important considerations which affect the software development environment; see Table 1.2.

The emphasis on good software is altered by the above considerations, as they change the strategy of 'software production' to that of 'software development'; from central control knows best despite what the user and developers know, towards a distributed responsibility centred on what the end user wants. There is also a move away from the deskilling of the programmer's work, by way of the evolution of the 'software engineer' or developer who is conversant with all phases of the development task and in close contact with the end user. By using a suitable development method, and having close contact with the end user, there is an improvement in software quality.

Table 1.2

Factors Affecting Software Development

Main Factors

The people that are to develop the product.
The work environment in which they develop the soft
ware.
The methodologies and tools that they use.
The need to produce quality software.

Subsidiary factors

The politics of the organisation.
The need for experimentation and error.
The appointment of the correct person as development
controller.
The psychology of the team members.
The need for standardisation.

The need for this increase in user involvement also implies that the central control needs to be modified. The usual development environment needs to be changed, and the attitudes of the development team members and management need to adapt to this environment. The environment needs to have a greater flexibility in terms of where the work is done, hours worked, methods of working, and methods of control. To do this there needs to be at the disposal of the software engineer a variety of automated tools, and an associated set of development methods. However, too much diversification can lead to chaos, so a compromise must be reached, and the set of 'tools' chosen and agreed in advance by the development team. Furthermore, there is also a need for continual upgrading of skills and consideration of new ideas and facts, i.e. a need for experimentation and research, which is also part of the development, rather than the production strategy.

The need for control of the projects must be centred on the teams that actually perform the tasks, with the addition of a development controller who oversees the development tasks from a strategic point of view. The day to day control is therefore vested in the development team, and the managerial control in the development controller. Such an appointment is critical to the success of such a development strategy, and the candidate must have the relevant depth of technical knowledge and sufficient management skill, to cope with a flexible environment.

The last consideration is the attitude of the organisation to the DP function within it, i.e. the 'politics'. Some modification of the command structure of the organisation is necessary in order that a 'software engineering' environment can survive and flourish. This is bound up with the effectiveness of the DP department, and who the manager of that department reports to. In recent years the cost of equipment and the control the DP function has on an organisation's health have caused the DPM (Data Processing Manager) either to become a board member or to report directly to a board member. The DP department that is seen as an extension of the accounts department or of other functional areas of the organisation will fail to provide the required environment. The move away from the traditional roots is to be welcomed if this leads to a greater awareness of the DP task in other organisational sectors, and the adoption of the dynamic user centred approach. Hence, systems engineering is the scientific planning, design, evaluation and construction of a human-machine interface, such that that interface is specific to the task in hand, and complements the human counterpart. (The name 'DP department' is used for convenience – it could equally well be called an Information Services Group in a different context.)

Summary

The idea of what a system is, and the basic types of system has been introduced, along with the system life cycle and the development stages of a software system. This leads to the idea of resources being used to produce a system, and a measure of the costs at each stage of the life cycle.

A discussion of what is still going wrong with software development followed, along with a consideration of the environment needed to correct matters. This can be summed up as a move away from the production centred environment, with little or no end user involvement, towards a dynamic development centred environment with considerable user involvement, and enhancement of development team skills.

Exercises

1) Write down the stages a system goes through, and try to identify how much end user input there is in each stage.

2) Using the example of the event diary, make a list of possible extensions you would like to see. If you were the end user, you have essentially written down the end user requirements for the proposed system.

3) Using the list from question 2 consider the points one by one, and try to assess which areas would be the most difficult to implement.

References

[1] Systems Behaviour, Open Systems Group, Open University, ISBN 006-318212-2.

[2] A Behavioural Theory of Management, Academy of Management Journal, Dec. 67.

[3] A Daniels & D Yeates, Basic Systems Analysis, Pitman ISBN 0 273 02053 6, 1984.

[4] A Parkin, Edward Arnold, Systems Analysis, ISBN 0 7131 2800 3, 1980.

[5] Introducing Systems Analysis, NCC publications.

[6] Estimating Software Costs, Datamation Sept, Oct, Nov 79.

[7] L.H. Putnam & A Fittzsimmons, The Dimensions of Maintenance, Proceedings of the Second International Conference on Software Engineering, IEEE, Oct 76 pp 492-497.

[8] B. Boehm, Software Engineering Economics, Prentice Hall 1981, ISBN 0 13 8221227.

[9] B. Boehm, Software Reliability – Measurement and Management, Abr Proc AIAA Software Mgmt Conference, Los Angeles, Jun 76.

2

Methods, Models and Prototyping

Objectives

Define the concepts of system modelling.

List the main prototyping methods

Describe how they can be used to develop systems.

Modelling and Systems

The first chapter identified some of the characteristics of a system, and outlined the way that a proposed computer system tried to map the existing manual or computer system in its method of working. To produce the computer system in its necessary complexity, it is required that the person or people who produced the said computer system, thoroughly appreciate the workings and complexity of the system. If the system is large, then this task is extremely difficult. Most people tend to simplify and make generalisations or 'rules of thumb' when coming to terms with a new problem. Often, when that problem is large and/or difficult, we make a model of the system or problem so that we can simulate it, and hence understand its behaviour.

The economy of building such a model is obvious, since it will be on a smaller and more manageable scale than the actual problem or system, and all configurations, alterations and behaviour can be tested and simulated on the model. Finally, the actual model forms the basis of discussion, measurement and simulation of the system rather than the system proper, hence reducing costs, and improving the reliability and design of the final system. The idea of building a model of the system is a direct transfer from engineering, whereby the engineer will build a scale model of components, and finally a prototype of the finished product which to test. The behaviour of the prototype is then examined and set against the design criteria outlined in the original product specification. The formulation of design criteria for engineering and software construction are similar, the only difference being that it is somewhat easier to put quantitative measures on reliability, performance and price on mechanical objects. Even so the product still has to be tested, and evaluated prior to release.

Table 2.1

Why Build Models?

Inevitable: There are no fixed or permanent dividing lines between facts about a system, and the beliefs held about a system or situation. Models are theories, laws, equations or beliefs which state things about the problem in hand, and assist in our understanding of it.

Economic: The compression of a system into model form allows information to be passed, assessed and quantified, so that the ideas and beliefs contained within the model can be altered or modified at will.

Simulation: When we build a model, of necessity we over-generalise and simplify. This is to make clear those complex areas within the task at hand, and to enable an economy of scale to take place. By simplification we can ensure a close examination of those parts of the system that may prove contentious, or where an improvement in existing working is required.

Thus, if we build a model we have an aid to problem solving, more specifically in terms of the computing environment.

❏ Classification of the system area or reference via the software engineers' internal knowledge and bias

❏ The encoding of the system elements into familiar concepts and ideas

❏ Formation of the system elements into structural patterns and representations (e.g. outline menus and processing elements).

Types of Model

There are various types of model which we can create for a given circumstance. The choice of which representation is dependent on the system we are trying to model, and the purpose of that model. Table gives a brief description of the types of model we can construct.

Table 2.2

Types of Model

Descriptive models: These provide a qualitative description and explanation of the system we are considering.

Predictive models: These are produced so that estimates of performance, cost and degrees of accuracy may be accessed.

Mechanistic models: Are a description of the behaviour of the system, given inputs, outputs and processing requirements.

Empirical/statistical models: Are obtained by fitting data obtained from existing systems to paper and mathematical models.

Steady state models: These model the systems average performance against time.

Dynamic models: The model fully represents the fluctuations of performance with time.

Local models: These are a description of the individual subsystems that form the model, and hence the system.

Global models: A description of the whole of the model, and hence the system.

Systems Engineering can use many or all of the above types of model in the generation of a working understanding of the system or problem under consideration. There are however certain aspects that can be extracted from the above table that help us to formulate a suitable model that can be used with effect in an Systems Engineering Methodology (SEM). The characteristics we look for in our models are:

❑ A reflection in the representation of the real world properties of the system, and an accurate portrayal of the characteristics of the real world system.

❑ They are built in a standard and disciplined manner in accordance with some methodology.

❑ The complexity of the model is handled by suitable tools.

When we build models, the form or format of the information which is used to convey the result is important to the finished product. The planning, directing and executing of the operations or activities involved in the selected methodology is equally important. Also of equal importance is the assistance that the chosen methodology gives in getting started, and stepping through the development. The process of modelling is crucial to the quality of results. Finally, it must be apparent when the process is complete.

The model itself can be in the form of a concrete example, or an abstract declaration of behaviour. The form the model takes will vary between these extremes, but should be a basis for understanding the user's requirements, and the essential properties of the system. The model representation can, therefore, be viewed as a set of languages, e.g. graphical, structured English, mathematical and so on. These provide a representation of the system that we can think about and communicate to others, as well as modify and experiment with.

Traditional methodologies generate paper models of the existing systems. These are manipulated by the systems analyst to form a design which can then be coded into a working system. The idea behind this is that the paper model of the system is developed incrementally by the analyst in conjunction with the end user. Often, despite the implied interaction with the end user the final product does not meet requirements. This is problematic of current SEMs. One critical reason is that the models we build as software engineers must be accessible to the end user, and the notation and description of the proposed solution must be presented in a user-understandable form. We have, therefore, an amalgamation of the 'real world' problem; the software engineer's understanding of that system and the user's needs and requirements. See Figure 2.1. To match them is the purpose of the SEM.

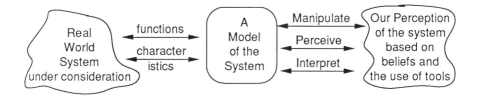

Figure 2.1 A Model is our Interface to the real world System

Creating a Model

The act of creating a model in SEM is an iterative and adaptive process. The model should, therefore, contain all the desired information on a given system in a readable and usable form. The following set of documentation is suggested as a starting point:

❏ A description of the desired system, so that the hardware, and software can be identified, evaluated and chosen.

❑ A system description so development costs can be estimated and accounted for.

❑ A consensus on system requirements prior to the generation of a formal requirements specification.

The viewpoint of the model must be flexible so as to encompass the system user or operator, the system implementor or maintainer, and finally the manager of the implementation project team. This assumes that the project is medium to large-scale. For the small project it will probably be necessary only to obtain user requirements as a starting point, and develop only critical areas of the problem into a full-blown specification. The production of a model is thus simplified, and the documentation is smaller and compact. Thus the structure of the documentation and the project team is dependent on problem size, in addition to our understanding of the problem.

The project team is of fundamental importance in the SEM. The tasks it has to complete are both necessary and complex, and can be stated as a set of aims as follows:

Table 2.3

Tasks of the Project Team

❑ Ensure that the model building is done by design, rather than by accident, and that there is a sense of purpose to the project, as well as a set direction. This produces the model as quickly and as cheaply as possible

❑ The team must formally combine the specialisations and expertise in the group, and the areas of specialisation within the system.

❑ Make certain that the work is concentrated on the critical areas of the project that are identified by overall economic criteria. However, it must also be aware that the best models are simple.

❑ Decide when the model reflects the system it is intended to represent. That is, it is adequate for the purpose intended, and that it is possible to predict overall system performance.

❑ Start and maintain a fruitful dialogue with the users of the system as early as possible in the project. This should help the other tasks that the model builders have to perform, as well as building confidence in the end user, as the project progresses.

❑ The remaining project team tasks are, specifically, the system requirement specification, system analysis and design, (within the prototyping framework) and final completed system release.

User Requirements

This relates how the project should reflect the requirements of the user – in other words, the specification, feasibility and user requirements for a particular project. In the previous section we saw that we can build models which help us determine the characteristics of user requirements. These characteristics have to be carried forward in a form that is able to reflect the complexity and subtlety of the problem in hand. It often takes the form of some sort of documentation, which allows the project team to work on the problem, and the user to identify with some of the technical requirements. The form this documentation may take is varied, and often depends on local working practices and standards. Indeed, there are several published sets of national standards, which may be adhered to when undertaking projects.

The requirements are obtained from the user by the project manager or team leader by building a model, using some form of methodology to elicit the facts from the end user, and can be seen as a clear follow on from the description of the model if used. The IEEE gave a definition of requirements in (IEEE ANSI 1981):

The requirements specification shall clearly and precisely describe the essential functions, performances, design constraints, attributes, and external interfaces. Each requirement shall be defined such that its achievement is capable of being objectively verified by a prescribed method, for example, inspection, demonstration, analysis or test.

Table 2.4

Requirements Documentation

❑ Introduction and guide to the requirements

❑ Summary of project characteristics

❑ Input, output and storage of data items

❑ Modes of operation of the system

❑ Performance requirements, i.e. timings, accuracy, error handling

❑ References and bibliography

There has been considerable concern on the part of DP professionals that the initial requirement specification will normally have to alter as the project progresses. There is no fundamental problem in this, providing we accept that the commercial and business environment is dynamic, and needs to be adaptive to external influences. The above definition implies that the requirements specification needs to be fixed. By using the correct methods to develop software the definition is just as valid for a dynamic approach to software development as it is to the production approach. There are four identifiable themes in a Systems Engineering Methodology (SEM) see also Figure 2.2:

❏ Separation of 'what' from 'how'

❏ Formalised specification of requirements as above

❏ Use of abstraction and information structures, which can be based on those used to develop a system model

❏ Documentation used as the design medium, using a variety of methods including graphics, English and mathematical symbols.

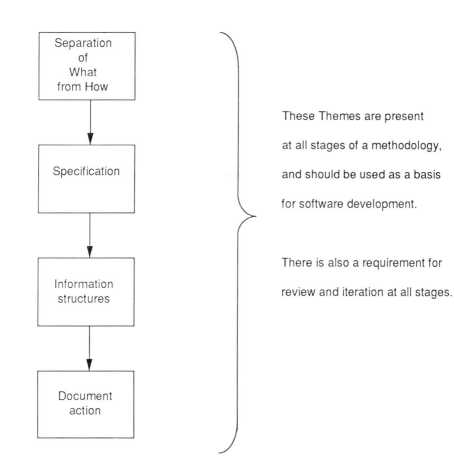

Figure 2.2 Systems Engineering Themes

Separation of What from How

The 'what' is the project's characteristics, and the functions applied to inputs to produce the outputs. As an example, consider our diary of events. There are three main functions that we may wish to perform on the contents of the diary:

❏ Input of a new event

❏ Change the event details

❏ Delete the event.

The data has to be accepted in some form, analysed for correctness and stored in a data store (file). The user must be able to input data in a normal way. Often in a diary system the event is 'pencilled in', and is then confirmed as correct at a later date. We must be able to allow the user to do this. The system will have to be as easy to use as a diary, or wall board, as well as offering further diary facilities to the user.

The contents of each function, and the data it handles, can be specified in detail. That is, the data items used by the function are identified and described in a fixed manner, and the function's actions are again described in further detail. Hence we have a set of levels or stages in development in which the detail and amount of knowledge we possess increases steadily as we study the system and its model. It is obvious that this process is not linear, and from time to time there will be a need to back track and re-evaluate the problem at its requisite development stages. The further 'down the line' the project is, the costlier this re-evaluation and correction becomes.

Formal Specification

The example of the diary is a fairly simple idea, but we can use it to determine the character of other software systems, and how we can identify what we need to make the formal specification work. In a formal specification there is a need to use Structured English and suitable graphics to describe the model to the user. Therefore, the model description must use a restricted and structured language in its content.

Table 2.5 identifies the main headings of a formal specification. This is then used as a working document, and can be discussed and analysed by the project team in conjunction with the end user.

Information Structures

The idea of 'information structures' comes from the fact that commercial DP systems process data in some form, from which information is obtained either directly by the system, or by interpretation by the end user. The computer systems purpose is to process and make available data in a form suitable for the end user. All computer systems have at their heart three main sections which differ in complexity and size from system to system.

Table 2.5

Software Systems Specifications

Environment and system interfaces: Is the system under consideration part of a wider system, and how does it fit in with existing systems, and the environment of its intended use?

Functions of The System: What the system attempts to do, and how the user interacts with it.

System performance: A measure of the speed, throughput, accuracy and reliability. The number and amount of resources the system will require during operation.

Operational requirements: How the system is maintained and used so that this is carried out properly.

Development schedule and cost: The time it is going to take to develop the system, and the cost of development.

The data that is accepted by the system can be in many forms, e.g. typed in at a keyboard, or from remote analog sensors. Similarly, the output can be presented in human understandable form, or in machine readable form, e.g. graphs, printouts, lights and control signals. The processing function transforms the said input to the said output, often performing calculations, sorts, searches and the like as it does so.

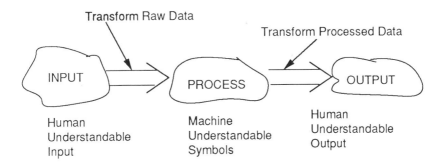

Figure 2.3 Simple Picture of a Computer System

As an example, consider a customer order. A typical one will have the customer's name and address, possibly with telephone number, and a set of items that the customer wishes to purchase. Within the computer system itself the same customer can have many orders which are current, some of which may be part filled, while others may still be waiting for processing.

We can state some of the simpler requirements for a computer system directly from this example, and by adding further requirements from fundamental knowledge related to what we may know about customer orders and order processing in particular arrive at the following:

❑ From the input (the order) we can obtain the customer's name address, and details of the order.

❑ Further to the pieces of information above we can perform other tasks which add to the content of the information:

> i) By knowing the customer's name and address we can do a check on credit rating, and also determine if they are a new or existing customer, either on our existing customer file, or via a credit checking system.

> ii) Similarly the customer could have an account. Has it been paid? Is there a credit note pending? Is he/she a good payer?

> iii) The items themselves can also produce information about stock levels, availability, part orders, and the customer's purchasing requirements and purchasing patterns, which is important if we sell seasonal goods, or perishable items.

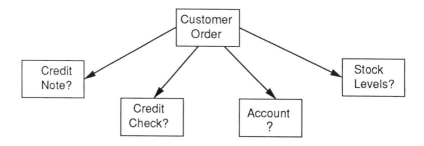

Figure 2.4 Extra Information needed before processing a customer order

Documentation as a Design Medium

The act of collecting forms, and example inputs and outputs, as well as constructing a model of the system on paper causes us to choose some form of written representation. Even at the model stage the structure of the documentation for the project should take on a shape and form.

Section 1: An introduction and background to the project, containing a system outline and definitions of any terms to assist reading the documentation.

Section 2: Data descriptions of input and output, example forms (if any), sets of data and intermediate data forms. Eventually as the project develops, this section takes the form of a data dictionary or information store.

Section 3: Operation, and information flow through the system, as defined at present, and eventually the new proposed system.

Section 4: Cost benefit analysis, system requirements, accuracy, and reliability estimates. Again, this is developed as the project progresses.

This representation can be carried over to prototyping, and machine representations using the automated tools now available. Even if we have to perform the task manually we can still use the framework for development, and by selection of the correct representations, be they graphical or textual, the end result is a set of working documents that are used as part of the design process itself.

Prototyping

"A quickly developed working model of the final system, which displays the majority of the required system's functionality".

The prototype must, therefore, have enough flexibility to respond to changes in the user requirements, and in the design due to errors and omissions from the initial user specification.

There is considerable misunderstanding of the use of prototyping in the computer industry. This can be traced back directly to the production environment of the structured methodologies, and the perceived 'need for control' required by programming management. What, therefore, are the worries that a development department may have when using a prototyping method?

Most of the current methods of working have at their root some form of project control, costing, and the identification of milestones, i.e. three months into project XYZ we shall have designed the file system and input modules. Most managers like to see this sort of concrete performance out of a project team. However, three months down the line of the project development the user requirements may alter, and he/she may wish to add another type of record, and alter the content of a few of the existing records, thereby altering the requirements. The project team may have already generated all the code that may no longer work. The result is that the project slips; it gets delayed! What is needed, therefore, is a method by which the end user can be included throughout the project. They can see what they are going to get at an early stage in the development. Using a prototyping method we can develop the system alongside the design.

Table 2.6

Prototyping Myths

❏ Prototyping leads to loss of project control, due to its flexibility, lack of clear milestones and deliverables.

❏ Prototyping is only suitable for trivial applications. This implies small and low-cost non-strategic projects.

❏ Prototyping is unstructured and undisciplined; this follows on from the first comment.

❏ Prototyping is a single development methodology.

Parallel Development of the Prototype with the Design

The goal of any prototyping method is to produce a system that is consistent with business requirements. The commercial pressures of business are dynamic, and therefore cannot be placed in the 'straight jacket' of traditional development methods, and fixed specifications – hence prototyping and dynamic SEMs.

Table 2.7

Development of prototypes – the alternatives

Illustration of system	vs.	Use of system
Interface	vs.	Interface + core
Keep it	vs.	Throw it away
Keep prototype	vs.	Keep Data Dictionary
Incremental	vs.	Iterative
Continuous	vs.	Staged

Often the basis of a prototyping system is a database (DB) or data dictionary (DD). The system we are prototyping consists of the interface (input, output, and possibly some processing modules or functions). The core of the system is, therefore, the DB or DD. The development of the system is iterative, in that it repeats several stages, each time gaining in detail and user functionality.

Table 2.8

The Pros and Cons of Prototyping

Plus Points

❏ Most operational shortcomings can be found early in the development of the system and are, therefore, eliminated.

❏ The user has to be closely involved in the project for prototyping to work successfully.

❏ It is fast and relatively inexpensive.

Minus Points

❏ Prototyping is normally done around specific 4GLs and the associated Data Dictionary.

❏ The systems analysis methodologies available do not link business analysis and an organisation's strategic planning.

❏ It is difficult to run in parallel with traditional structured methods of program development.

Prototyping Method

The method of system prototyping is deceptively simple on paper, there being essentially four steps:

❏ Production of a document that defines the content of the project, (User Requirements).

❏ Split the system up into core and peripheral modules.

❏ Produce the core modules and get them working first; then produce the peripheral modules.

❏ Iterate by adding changing requirements, and further definition of the system and user requirements.

Management Issues

The decision to prototype:

❑ Whether to prototype at all

❑ The approach to prototyping and which method to adopt

❑ What parts of the system to prototype.

Planning:

❑ Formulation of aims and ideas for the prototype and the project

❑ Staff selection

❑ Tool selection (development tools)

❑ Budgeting and scheduling of project

❑ User commitment and time-scale.

Control:

❑ When is prototyping cut off or finished?

❑ How to evaluate and propagate change.

Documentation:

❑ Of the prototyping process

❑ Of changes in the documentation.

The production of the project's requirements is dealt with in the previous section, and should be matched closely with the requirements analysis, with the proviso that it is bound to change due to business pressures and environmental factors. (If the project is non-trivial.) Hopefully, a prototyping systems engineering method will cope and have a complementary flexibility.

The system is split up into a core series of modules, from which we hang or attach modules that use the core modules, or are driven by them. The 'core system development' should contain:

❑ The modules of the core

❑ The initial file layouts (DD or DB)

❑ The file maintenance functions

❑ Specific critical technical areas, e.g. intermachine communications.

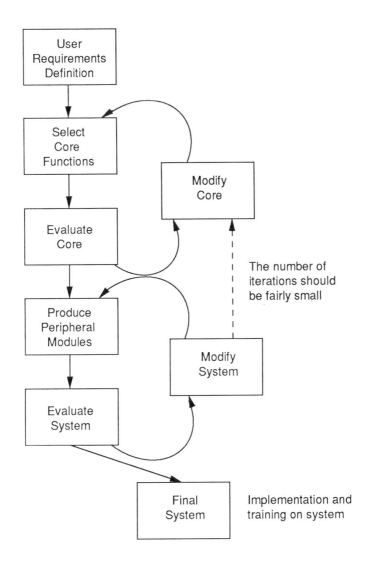

Figure 2.5 System Prototyping Method

The aim of producing a working core is to define a minimum working system. This can be further developed in close consultation with the user. It also provides a structure on which performance can be assessed.

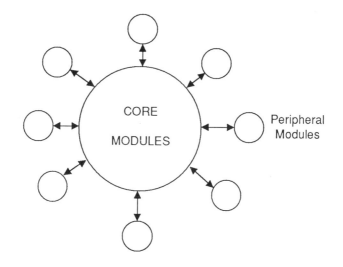

Figure 2.6 Outline System

After the production of the core set of modules, further sections or modules are selected from major to minor. This allows 'what' to be solved rather than 'how'. Problems are solved as the project progresses; testing and error correction are performed on the production of each module, and a working system is available to the user at all times so that feedback is immediate. This allows any errors, omissions and additions to be considered and discussed by the customer (the user) with the project team and, hopefully, added to the proposed system.

The benefits of prototyping can be numerous and, specifically, split into two groups, the technical benefits (Table 2.9), and the benefit of increased user involvement (Table 2.10).

Construction of a Prototyping Methodology

In the previous pages I have outlined sets of considerations which must be taken into account prior to the adoption of a suitable prototyping method. One fundamental characteristic is the type and value of the 'tools' available to the developer. Normally, as a developer becomes more skilled at the task, the 'tool set' used becomes limited to those that they can use easily, and that give the best results for themselves. However, this may not be adequate for the purposes of serious development. The outline prototyping method identified earlier gives a view of the development method which is used. These, coupled with the management issues, should give us the necessary structure to our development/prototyping methodology.

Initially at least, the type of project we wish to prototype and develop dynamically should be well chosen, so as to use a well understood problem; possibly one that has already been solved in the form of an existing computer system. The planning requirements will, therefore, be easier to obtain, as they will be based on the existing system. The selection of the staff is crucial at this point. Since the traditional DP department is isolationist, native members of staff from that department will have to be weaned away from a production role into the user-centred development role, which is a necessary part of this prototyping method.

Table 2.9

Technical Benefits of Prototyping

❏ The project team has to perform programming, analysis and design. Therefore, each individual team member will find it necessary to understand what they are attempting to achieve. Team members can design code and test modules in the prototype, with the rest of the team or as separate entities.

❏ Support of the system is no longer dependent on one person.

❏ Maintenance of the system is no longer dependent on one person.

❏ There is an increase in motivation, and removal of boredom.

❏ The time period for development is collapsed, since problems are solved as they arise.

❏ The prototyping of a system implies modern languages and design tools.

❏ It is easy to develop the prototype into the release system proper if later versions of programming languages are used in the production of software.

Table 2.10

Customer Involvement In Prototyping

❏ All issues and problems are visible from early on in the project.

❏ The project's progress is easily checked with the targets that are spelled out in the requirements document.

❏ The functionality of the system can be controlled.

❏ The implementation can be modified if requested by the user.

❏ The project team and the customer become knowledgeable about the system.

❏ The final customer training is smoother and speedier.

The control of the development can be done in several ways. One of the best is to outline the user requirements in some form, either on paper or on a machine, i.e. general screen and menu layouts with descriptions of operations performed on the data. Then, in conjunction with user reaction, develop and refine these so they give the correct response. Secondly, produce outline reports which can be changed in accordance with user wishes, and lastly, provide the support facilities and aids for use, such as program back-up, on-line help and a training pack. At this stage the development should be considered complete, and as such, be handed over to the user.

If one reads the various articles and references, we can see various methods by which we can adopt a prototyping methodology for our systems development. However, if we consider the developments being made in software, then the use of code-generators and very high level languages allows us to build a usable customer interface as well as the underlying logic simply and easily from the initial requirements. As the initial requirements are enhanced (understood), we enhance the prototype to include extra or changed requirements. As the process is dynamic, and the change-over between prototype and actual system becomes blurred, it is probably incorrect to take a fixed view and model of what is essentially a systems engineering task.

Summary

The problems associated with prototyping have, to some extent, stopped organisations adopting it. This has been due to a misunderstanding on the part of development managers who believe that software control is invested in closely defined production methodologies rather than a dynamic relationship between developer and user. However, as modern development tools become widespread, and user departments become responsible for the production of their own software the development process is seen as one of support and guidance of end users rather than control. Subsequently, the adoption of prototyping by an organisation can lead to a greater awareness of user needs, an improvement in design, and production of the required systems, as well as a reduction of the maintenance burden. There is also a parallel development in languages which will take high-level definitions and transform them into code for execution and interpretation, so that a full spectrum of development tools is now available, and there is little excuse for using traditional methods unless we have to do so.

Exercises

1. Consider the following diagram:

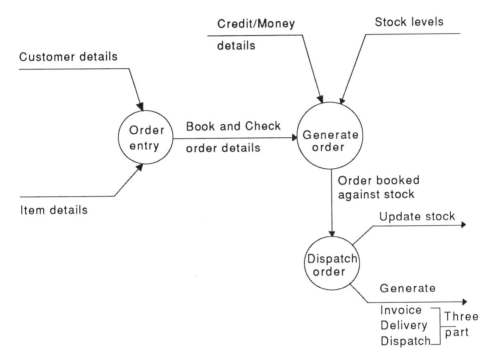

a. The customer orders can either be satisfied from stock or bought in specially. Where do we need to consider this?

b. Sketch out possible screens and reports/outputs needed.

2. Obtain one of the proprietary database packages and evaluate it for ease of development of screens, reports and logic. Compare this with a high-level language with which you are familiar. You should find that the handling package allows a considerably condensed development schedule.

References

[1] L. McNish, Consider Prototyping for your next project, DEC USER May 1988, pp 25-26.

[2] D. Ince, Getting it right first on the drawing board, Systems International Feb 88, pp 55,56,58.

[3] P. Checkland, Systems Thinking and Practice, Wiley 1981, ISBN 0471279110

[4] E. Mumford, F.F. Land and J. Hawgood, A Participative approach to the design of computer systems, Impact of science on society Vol 28 No3.

[5] P.J. Mayhew P.A. Dearnley, An Alternative Prototyping Classification, The Computer journal, Vol 30, No 6 1987.

[6] D. C. Ince and S. Hekmalpour, Software Prototyping in the Eighties, Information Technology Briefings.

[7] P.E. Bates, Prototyping: A Motivation, Seminar Series on New Directions in Software Development. Wolverhampton Polytechnic April 1989.

3

Analysis and Design

Objectives

Describe analysis and design methods

Show how they are tailored to fit particular problems.

Systems Analysis and Design Methods

The first point to make when discussing analysis and design methods is that there are as many methods as there are analysts. Most people develop their problem solving ability over many years, and develop a sort of sixth sense. The knowledge they possess is probably not in the form of a set of rules or check lists such as are often given in systems analysis books. However, having said that, the knowledge of how to solve a problem is not rule based, and tends not to be user centred. How can we can fit methodologies into the concept of prototyping, and increased customer participation?

I present two methodologies in outline, which combined together allow the analyst to construct a well designed system, prior to coding. Other methods can be substituted. [2,10,11,12,13]. I have found that these, coupled with good documentation and an environment that allows prototyping, provide a good basis for system development.

Checkland's Soft Systems Methodology

This methodology tackles problems centred around what are called 'human activity systems' so that the ideas that were introduced in the earlier chapters can be used to structure and describe problems, and control and understanding can take place [9].

Most modern computer systems have at the 'front end' some form of sophisticated user interface. They also attempt to computerise the non-trivial manual processing systems, or systems that have been partly computerised. Therefore, there is still a need for a high level of user interaction with the system. Hence it would automatically benefit from a user centred prototyping SEM.

The analyst is presented with a system which is not clearly definable in terms of functions and data stores, or indeed procedures, for information analysis. It is, therefore, a system that displays most of the attributes of an open/soft system. Analysis of the situation attempts to identify three components, structure and process.

The structures of the situation and the process are complex interactions; they are concerned with what resources are deployed in what operational area under what planning procedures, in what environment, and by whom, and how this deployment is monitored and controlled. To enable the formation of a solution the analyst will propose a model of the system, which is then discussed with the customer. This then provides a definition of the actual system, which can then be further developed, (i.e. model to prototype to system).

The organisational layout and structure of the system is based on the management hierarchy, the position of equipment, people and resources. In other words, the physical environment in which the system will operate.

The reporting and communicational structure of the organisation is the method by which control is exercised in the system. It is usually split into two; the internal and external activities concerned with monitoring and planning.

Finally, an attempt is made to identify the high-level goals of the analysis. Typically these can be tied in with company policy, and organisational requirements.

Coupled to these are factors such as staff motivation, financial measures of performance, cost, value, benefit and profit.

After a model is made of the proposed system, this is discussed and compared with the user's ideas on what the system is intended to do. From this discussion, or set of discussions, an accepted definitive description of the system is produced. This stage is a comparison of the definitions or possible solutions of the problem at hand. Not what 'ought to be'! The result comes from a client/analyst discussion regarding the structure, organisation and contents of the system model. Using the model, an agreement can be formulated, which allows any proposed organisational changes to be studied,and the amount and degree of computerisation to be discussed and taken a stage further to formal analysis and design using the prototyping method as outlined.

Obviously, the amount of work that is performed at the preliminary stage is dependent on the size of the project, and a rough idea of the resources available.

Table 3.1 Discussion Environment

Measure of System Objectives

❑ Throughput of the proposed system.(Hit rate, transaction rate, query processing response time). Qualitative measures of the performance of the existing system, against those in the proposed notional system.

❑ Justifications based on costs, equipment savings, wage costs, accommodation costs and improvement in management information.

System Attributes

❑ The system's man machine interface, i.e. is it proposed that the system is screen, icon and window driven?

❑ How much is left to user discretion and involvement?

❑ Does it fit in with the existing procedure, or replace it?

System Functions

❑ Identification of functions and tasks that need to be done by the system. (Accept client name and address, create new record if client is new, otherwise check contents.)

❑ Assignment of data stores for information.

❑ Process control structures, and reporting mechanisms.

❑ Organisational requirements and structures.

Once the model has been agreed, the system can be designed to meet the requirements of the model. This can be done in several ways. Perhaps one of the best is SSADM (Structured Systems Analysis and Design Method). There are several books that are available on this subject so it will not be explained more fully her, but will be the basis of an example problem. For a fuller discussion see [14,15].

SSADM (Structured Systems Analysis and Design Method)

This was developed originally for the UK Government by a company called Learmouth and Burchett Management Systems and the government's computer advisory body CCTA. It is now a mandatory standard for government projects.

As the name implies it looks only at the analysis and design of a project, by focusing on the use and analysis of data within a system. The detailed construction, testing and implementation is left to other methods; so is the early user requirements analysis and model building. Depending on the type and characteristics of the problem, SSADM can be used as it stands, or an analysis method such as Checkland's can be used to develop a model prior to commencement of analysis proper. The following table identifies the type of project that could benefit from using SSADM; all commercial projects with the usual time span of 18 months to 2 years will benefit.

Table 3.2 Using SSADM

Use where:

❑ The project is medium to large scale

❑ The project is expected to be of high cost

❑ There is a long projected time scale

❑ Strategic planning needs to be done

❑ Projects are sensitive to justification, or justification is in doubt.

Not advisable where:

❑ The project is small

❑ The project is expected to be low cost

❑ The projected time scale is of a small duration

❑ The project is developed as part of a larger strategy

❑ Some work has already been done on more traditional lines.

The break even point seems to be around one to two months duration. Below this time span the amount of work involved in performing the tasks in SSADM outweighs the benefits of adopting it. However, some of the techniques that are used in SSADM could be of use in these smaller projects, as an aid to development or as a guideline for documentation and development. Indeed, some of the diagramming techniques are of considerable value when discussing a project with the end user.

A recent survey showed that 46% of the UK's large installations used or planned to use SSADM or one of the variants. The National Computing Centre (NCC) has attracted large numbers of companies to seminars on SSADM, and the take up of SSADM and other structured method courses given by NCC and other training companies is expected to increase. The strengths of SSADM lie in the computerisation of existing systems, and the control and analysis of the design phase. The first chapter introduced the concept of a typical commercial DP system, and its attributes of 'hard and semi closed', i.e. the system is well defined, and is in a finite boundary, and its properties, processes and functions are readily identifiable – hence the analysis is easily done. Where this is not the case, and strategic or business planning have to be taken into consideration, then a pre-stage of analysis may be necessary to identify the system and form of the model proper, which can then be enhanced and continued by SSADM.

Table 3.3

Factors leading to the adoption of SSADM

❑ It is a well documented method, and is supported by a variety of training and consultancy firms

❑ There are a number of 'tools' that support and enhance its use

❑ The documentation and training allow a 'cook-book' approach

❑ It can be introduced to new projects easily, without the need to consider the processes and the run time environment

❑ It also allows the identification of control points for project management.

The introduction of computer tools has made the method easier to implement. These automate the tedious and time consuming parts of the method, by checking the method's validity as the analysis and design progresses through the stages. The whole method is based on a graphical representation of the system model, which is an aid to communication between the analyst and the end user. Figures 3.1a and 3.1b illustrate the stages in SSADM and contrasts it with the waterfall model of the system life cycle.

There are three types of graphical descriptions which can be presented within SSADM to represent the system model.

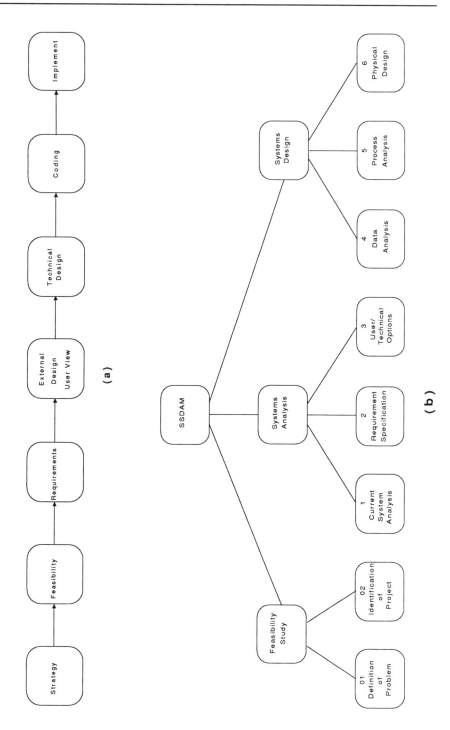

Figure 3.1 The SSADM hierarchy (a) compared with the System Life Cycle (b)

Firstly, the logical data structure, which provides a way of representing relationships between data elements in the system. This can be expanded via discussion with the user to a composite picture showing structure, data fields, access paths and volume information. The whole is analogous to a Data Dictionary, and can be used as such to design the physical database, which may be used by the system.

Secondly, flow diagrams are used to show the way that information is moved around the system, and which processes act on that information. These provide a good vehicle for discussion.

Thirdly, the entity life history shows the events affecting an entity during its life in the system. (When it is created, altered and deleted, for example.)

All of these can be presented in an automatic fashion to the analyst by suitable computer software, so that they can be expanded and developed as the project progresses. Coupled with a powerful code generator and prototyping system, they form a powerful development system. The diagrams mentioned above can also be drawn out by hand and used in isolation if so wished.

As an example of the use of the diagrams and aids, the following small project was completed in a little over 40 hours, using parts of the SSADM technique, and a proprietary database as the prototyping and development language.

Example Small System

The system was developed as an aid to the control and management of clerical procedures in a company which specialises in the house purchase market.

Initially the company's director wished to allow the company clerks to keep details of clients' house purchases on a database, which allowed the identification of each client, as well as the progress and prospective profit in each of the company's operating areas. The following were the minimum requirements of the company director (the user requirements.)

❏ Acceptance of client details.

❏ Identification of the area of the country in which the purchaser lived. (For the purposes of the exercise this will take in five areas.)

❏ Identification of the stage and date the purchase has reached.

❏ The client's insurer, building society, and the firm's consultant who deals with the particular client.

❏ The cost and type of any improvement, along with its supplier. (e.g. double glazing required.)

❏ A set of reports that would allow the individual identification of a client, and the stages at which the purchase had progressed, sorted by area, consultant, insurer, society and solicitor.

Notes

After further questions the following information was received:

The name of the company's operating areas: Sheffield, Blackburn, Midlands, Plymouth, Chelmsford

The purchase stages:

❏ The right to buy sent by the prospective purchaser to the council

❏ Awaiting mortgage application

❏ Awaiting home improvement survey

❏ Awaiting customer quotations for improvement

❏ Mortgage application to society made

❏ Mortgage offer from building society

❏ Legal completion of council house purchase

❏ Installation of improvement

❏ Re-inspection of property

❏ Financial completion.

The client had to be identified by a unique client code.

The whole system should be easy to use, and screen based as much as possible.

The data flow diagram can be drawn from these initial requirements, along with prospective data structure. Figures 3.2 and 3.3 illustrate this technique,.

The existing manual system also had a form that acted as a summary sheet for the client file. This was filled in as the prospective purchase went through the system (Figure 3.4.). From the initial discussion, and an analysis of the form's contents, an outline Data Dictionary was constructed, which acted as a model for the eventual system's database, with suitable additions. Table 3.3 is the DD for the house purchase system in its original model form.

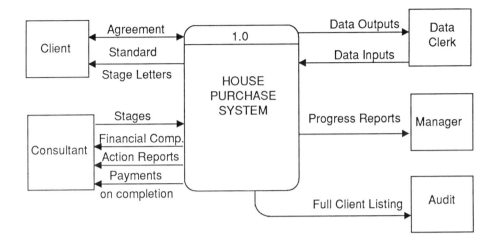

Figure 3.2 First Cut DFD for House Purchase System

Table 3.3 The proposed data dictionary

Field name	Type	Width	File	Reference
Client's first name	Char	20	Client	
Client's second name	Char	20	Client	
Client's title	Char	1	Client	ref1
Address line 1-3	Char	20	Client	
Client's postcode	Char	8	Client	
Client's telephone	Alpha/Num	14	Client	
Consultant	Char	20	Client	
Building society	Char	20	Client	
Client's solicitor	Char	20	Client	
Client's insurer	Char	20	Client	
Improvement type	Char	20	Client	
Supplier of improvement	Char	20	Client	
Quote from supplier	Numeric	7.2	Client	
Hire purchase	Numeric	7.2	Client	
Individual stages 1-10	Date	8	Client	ref2

ref1 *Client's title coded 1 for Mr, 2 for Ms and so on.*

ref2 *Date format dd/mm/yy. (There are ten of these!)*

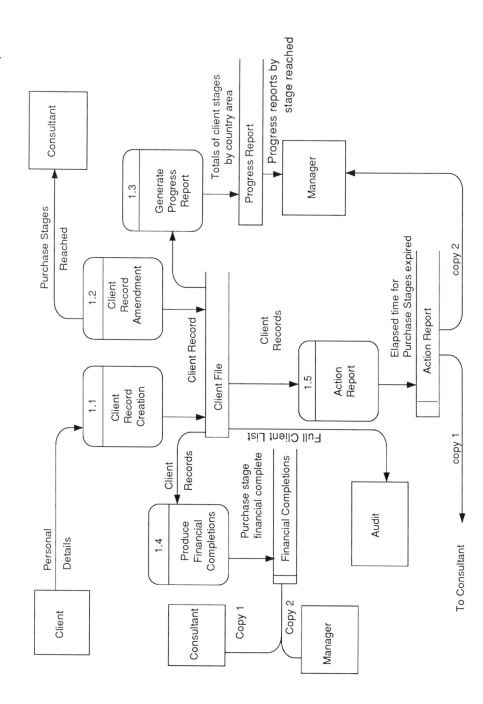

Figure 3.3 First Cut Second Level DFD for House Purchase System

Name:- _____   _____

Address _____   Phone _____

              _____

              _____

Consultant _____

Building Society _____

Solicitor _____

Insurer _____

House Improvement type _____

                           Quote £ _____

                           H.P.   £_____

Stages   Date

     Right to buy _____

     Awaiting Valuation _____

     Awaiting Home Improvement Survey _____

     Awaiting Customer Quotation _____

     Mortgage Application _____

     Mortgage Offer _____

     Legal Completion _____

     Installation _____

     Re Inspection of Improvement _____

     Final Completion _____

Notes _____

         _____

         _____

         _____

Figure 3.4 Client summary sheet

The diagrams and initial design were then discussed with the director of the company, and the following points raised:

❏ The action report was to be produced when specific time intervals elapsed at each of the stages. The individual times were as follows:

To receiving valuation	13 weeks
To receiving home improvement quote	2 weeks
To receiving final quote accepted by client	2 weeks
To submitting mortgage application	1 week
To receiving mortgage offer	1 week
To legal completion	3 weeks
To improvement being installed	6 weeks
To reinspection by Building Society	1 week
To financial completion	1 week

❏ The clients were accepted on to the system but did not seem to leave it! The clients left the system either at the end of the stages, i.e. at financial completion, or by cancellation of the contract.

❏ Each client needed a unique identification code or job number. A compound code was proposed that identified the area of the country, the date of the clients joining the scheme, and the job number on that particular day.

The job number then became the key field of the client's record:

First character	Alphabetic
Next six characters	Date
Last three characters	Numeric

eg C071187111 is Chesterfield district, the date 7th of November 1987, job number 111.

As the expected number of clients for each financial year was expected to be around 1,500 for the whole of the group, the key field should be able to uniquely identify the individual clients on the file.

❏ At the end of the financial year the company's auditors should be able to check the computer file against the company's documents. To do this they will need a complete print out of the file.

The data flow diagram and suggested data dictionary were altered accordingly, along with the suggested structure charts for the data. At this stage the prototype can be started, along with the system's detailed design. We already have the basic DD and an outline of what information needs to be presented to the data entry clerk from Figure 3.4. Similarly, the consultants need to know when a client has reached the stages, or is held up at a specific stage. Finally, at the end of the year the auditors must be able to follow a client through the system.

The report we have not discussed as yet is the company area progress report; this is important to management as it identifies the number of clients and stages reached for each company area. The structure of this report is shown in Figure 3.5. The DD is easily extended to show the required fields.

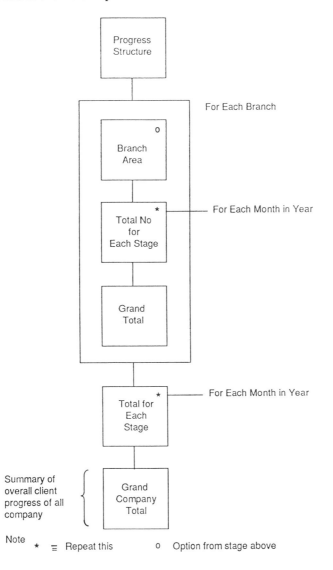

Figure 3.5 Company/client progress

System Design Methodologies

There are again numerous design methodologies to choose from, which can be used in conjunction with analysis methods or on their own. Some of these can be used in the framework of SSADM. The choice of design method is critical to the achievement of a 'good' system, especially when that system is developed using a prototype as the development vehicle [5,11,14,15]. The whole development process is outlined in Figure 3.6.

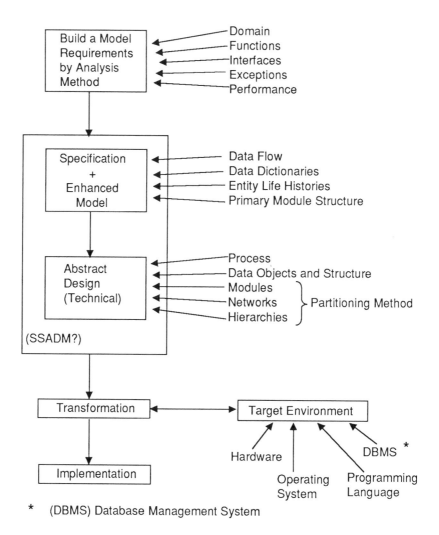

*   (DBMS) Database Management System

Figure 3.6 How it Fits Together

The diagram shows how the stages of the development process fit together, and the considerations which are used when undertaking the development. So far we have discussed a method of obtaining the requirement analysis and the specification. What, then, of the abstract specification? The detail contained in this depends on the formality of the specification required, and the complexity of the problem we are dealing with. The overall objective of any project is to meet user requirements, but as can be seen from the references given there are many ways of achieving this. However, since at this stage we are dealing with how we are to fit the processing logic into the system, here is a set of considerations which must be dealt with by any chosen design methodology. Table 3.4 identifies the considerations specific to design methods; Table 3.5 identifies what we should be attempting to achieve in terms of 'good software'.

Table 3.4 Design Stage Considerations

Process:
　The way that input data is transformed to output data.
　The application of formula functions and actions on the data to transform it from input to output.

Data Objects:
　The data items, stores, forms, printouts and screens.
　The contents, validation, range and requirements of data objects.

Partitioning Method:
　Modules: The splitting up of the system into suitable interconnecting sections ormodules, each specifically designed to perform a task.
　Networks: An abstract representation of the modules or functions, which show how the data moves through the system.
　Hirarchies: Called and calling sequence of modules in the system, determiningthe organisation of the system.

Finally, the difference between the analysis and the design phase is summed up by the following statement:

Systems Analysis is related to finding the 'what' and activities related to the 'what'. Systems Design is related to the 'How'.

Structured Design

Structured design attempts to formalise the partition of large complex systems on the lines given. The end result is a set of manageable sections or modules (sub-systems). Each relevant module has a set of characteristics, which are similar to the very simple system of input, process, output.

Table 3.5 Criteria for 'good' Software

Efficiency:
To make the best possible use of resources. The resources of the system are financial, technological, people and time. Over the last few years the most expensive resource has been people, rather than the hardware.

Reliability:
The end result of a design should be a reliable system. In hardware terms the MeanTime Before Failure (MTBF) should be long. There should be no serious problems if the design has been done correctly.

Maintainability:
The system should be easy to correct if there are any errors in it, and those errors should only affect a small amount of code.

Modifiability:
A commercial system needs to be dynamic, which implies that it is easy to modify,i.e. add bits to it, and to alter processes to reflect the changing environment.

Utility:
The human interface has to be good. In simple terms the system is easy to use, and consistent.

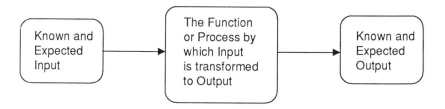

Figure 3.7 Characteristics of a subsection/Module

At this stage in the development of the example, the exact number and inner workings of each module are not known. However we do know that each will have an input, perform some processing and, eventually, output. This is a 'Black Box' approach – all we know about is the interface and the name of the module (input/output and function respectively). For our example, or indeed any project, we can split the system up into a set of modules that have an interface, and a name which identifies its function in the system. Most design methodologies partition the system into these small components and then attempt to reconcile the interfaces between them. The system is partitioned into modules via some set of rules which attempt to identify the module's interface, and functionality. For example:

❑ Each module should solve one well defined piece of the problem

❑ The function of each module should be understood, and obvious from its name, as should the partitioning

❑ Any connection between the modules is there only because there is a connection between the pieces of the problem

❑ The connections between modules are as simple as possible so that individual modules only deal with relevant pieces of data

❑ Control of modules is always performed by those higher in the design hierarchy.

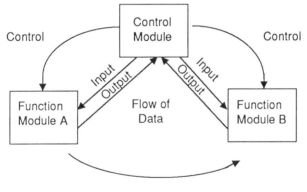

Logical Sequence

Figure 3.8 Representation of the design hierarchy

Some authors [16] classify the amount and strength of the module interface and this is called 'coupling'. The measure of coupling is dependent on how isolated the subordinate modules are from ones higher in the structure. Another measure of this interaction is 'cohesion' which again is a measure of the interaction between modules.

By using some further design considerations and a prototyping methodology, we can avoid much of the consideration of 'cohesion and coupling' between modules, by assuming a set of general considerations about systems and the design of modules.

Table 3.6 Further Design Considerations

Module size:	The size of the module should be sufficiently large to fulfil its purpose. The function should carry out one purpose. As a 'rule of thumb' one module per one sheet of printer paper.
Splitting:	The parts of the system can be split into sets of similar modules, e.g. data input, report generation/output.
Subordinates:	The optimum number of subordinate modules appears to be five or six. Beyond that the complexity of the control module becomes too great.
Generality:	Certain modules could be useful in more than one part of the system, e.g. a date calculation. This sort of module should be simple and as general as possible.
Balancing:	The overall shape of the system is important; generally, the number of modules concerned with input should be roughly equal to those which deal with output. The logic and working modules should be those which are lower in the hierarchy, and the control modules should be those higher.

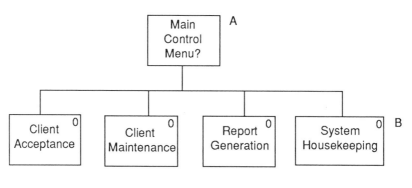

0   Option from stage A

Figure 3.9 Overall structure for the House Purchase Scheme

As an example, consider the House Purchase system. A first attempt at a structure for the program may be as in Figure 3.9 opposite.

The two modules, Report Generation and System Housekeeping, are sub control modules. The Report Generation module has control over the following reports:

❏ The action report (stage elapsed time exceeded)

❏ The cancellations (client cancels the purchase – Figure 3.10)

❏ The financial completion (purchase completed – Figure 3.11)

❏ The progress report.

Similarly, the System Housekeeping module deals with:

❏ Removal and archive of clients from the system

❏ Reindexing and backup of the system files

❏ Production of auditors' reports.

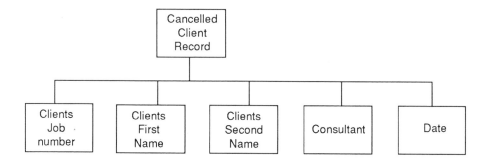

Figure 3.10 Cancellation Report Data Structure

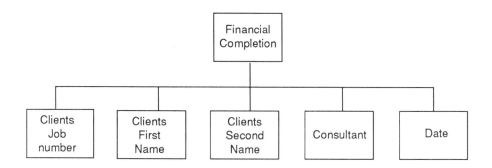

Figure 3.11 Financial completion report data structure

At first sight we have an unbalanced system. There are more modules concerned with output than there are for input. However we can analyse the structure of the required results. An example will do! If we examine the cancellation report, and the financial completion report, we find that the only difference is the report title and the criteria by which the client records are selected. Hence we can use the same module (reusability) with different control parameters, to select specific records and to put a different title on to the report. Furthermore, if we study each of the data structures of the other reports we should find similarities which we can then exploit when generating the code.

Summary

This chapter has been concerned with the SEM, and has introduced the idea that a framework of selected tools can help in the generation of software. Furthermore, when this is coupled with prototyping and customer involvement, we obtain an SEM that is flexible and dynamic enough to meet commercial situations. This has a degree of overlap and iteration built in – see Figure 3.12.

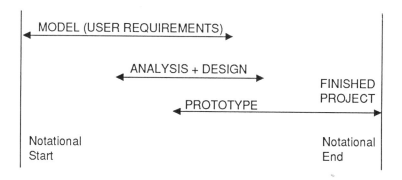

Figure 3.12 Overlap of the stages of development

If we adopt this SEM the stages are not clear cut, but can be identified. The important idea is that the model, analysis and design as well as the ongoing prototype are available to the customer (end user). This allows strong interaction, and discussion or adjustments to be made early in the project. The actual place where the project stops must also be agreed, as in any commercial system the requirements will alter with time. Hopefully by adopting the SEM as outlined above, the elapsed time between need and product will be shortened, and the changing business environment will not force many changes on the project. Since the project has been well designed and the user has had considerable input, the end result will be easy to modify, maintain and enhance as required, and hopefully provide what the user wants.

Exercises

1) Take the discussion with the director of the house purchase company, add the information given to the data flow diagram, and modify the data dictionary accordingly.

2) Identify the set of procedures the system will allow.

3) Complete the data structures of each report and data store. Check these against the data dictionary for any discrepancies.

4) Either sketch out, or use a screen painter, to outline the main menus and input screens.

References

[1] Yeh.R.T et al, Software requirements : New Directions and Perspectives, Handbook of Software Engineering, Van Norstrand Reinhold, New York 1984.

[2] R.H. Wallace et al, A Unified Methodology for Developing Systems, McGraw-Hill 1987.

[3] D. V. Steward, Software Engineering with Systems Analysis and Design, Brooks/Cole 1987.

[4] B. Ratcliff, Software Engineering: Principles and Methods, Blackwell 1987.

[5] R.S. Pressman, Software Engineering: A Practitioner's approach, McGraw-Hill 1987.

[6] M. L. Shooman, Software Engineering, McGraw-Hill 1983.

[7] E. Yourden, L. Constantine, Structured Design, Prentice- Hall, 1979.

[8] C. Gane, T. Sarson, Structured Systems Analysis, IST publications 1977.

[9] M Jackson, System Development, Prentice Hall, 1983.

[10] E. Downs, P. Clare, I Coe, Structured Systems Analysis and Design Method, Prentice Hall, 1988.

[11] G. Cutts, Structured Systems Analysis and Design Methodology Paradigm, 1987.

[12] Meiler Page Jones, Structured Design, ISBN 0-13-690777-6.

4

The Systems Designer's Environment

Objectives

Understand and appreciate the types and characteristics of design and development systems available.

Outline the component parts, and the operation of the design and development environment.

Appreciate the use of the environments in the production of software.

Describe the wider application environment of end users and organisational structure.

CASE and IPSE

This area of computer science is full of acronyms, and initials for products that are aids for the development of software. Essentially they all attempt to automate the automators. Until recently the productivity gains brought about by automation have been confined to areas other than DP. With the availability of products that automate the development of software, this is changing.

The products available cover three main areas:

❑ **4GL** (Fourth Generation Language): The languages COBOL and FORTRAN are third generation languages, and with the related structured design and development were the main software production tools of the 1970s.

❏ **CASE** (Computer Aided Software Engineering): The use of the computer to assist the software developer with the tasks of specifying requirements, design, documentation and generation of software.

❏ **IPSE** (Integrated Product Support Environment): This is aimed at providing the developer with a total environment. It includes project management, library, and system support. It can be likened to an operating system for development.

The purpose of CASE is to help the practitioner to develop computer-based solutions to systems in such a way that the said development is done as efficiently as possible. Presented to the developer is a set of tools, which steers him/her through the software life cycle, from initial request to final implemented solution. This means that the analysis, design and production can all be done using the sophisticated software ('tool box') that is available in a particular implementation of CASE. In this way the whole of the software life cycle can be automated whichever model of the life cycle we choose – be it the traditional 'waterfall' idea or a prototyping methodology.

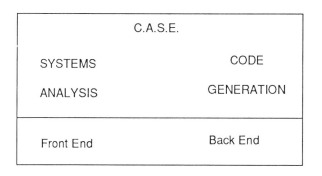

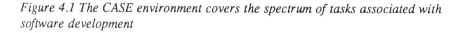

Figure 4.1 The CASE environment covers the spectrum of tasks associated with software development

The number of products available which support a full CASE environment are few. Most commercially available products are split into what are termed 'front ends' and 'back ends'. The 'front end' products aim to assist the developer in generating the requirements, and in the analysis of a system, and the 'back ends' assist the technical design and production of the system.

The IPSE and CASE environments operate within a particular model of the software development process. They support structured methodologies such as LSDM [1], SSADM [2], Yourden [3], Gane & Sarson [4] and Jackson [5]. In these methodologies a set of activities operated by the developer act on the objects (data reports, files and control functions) and produce a further set of objects. These final objects are often data flow diagrams, documentation, screen-layouts and other model forms.

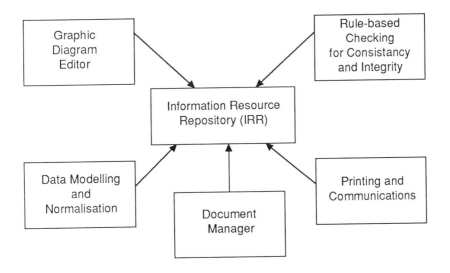

Figure 4.2 The components of CASE

The CASE environment supports several diagramming techniques:

❑ Data flow diagrams

❑ Data models

❑ Decomposition or tree structure diagrams

❑ Decision trees

❑ State transition diagrams.

'Rule-based' checking ensures that an entity is created, amended and deleted when it should; that the data structures contain relevant information; and that information can be obtained from the relevant source (input or data store). It can also perform checks on the contents of individual data fields to ensure the consistency of the data throughout the proposed system.

Data modelling and normalisation of the proposed systems data is crucial to the development. These modules in CASE allow the developer to construct data structures, views and stores of information. Normalisation of data tries to reduce redundancy and is closely analogous to the idea of normalisation in a relational database [6].

The document manager, printing and communications handle the management, output and compilation of the documents, diagrams and text produced by the CASE system.

The most important module in CASE is the Information Resource Repository. This stores the result of the analysis, and provides the database or data dictionary for subsequent code generation. This normally takes the form of a relational database [6] which acts as both the repository for design information, as well as a means of prototyping and development.

Table 4.1

Benefits of CASE

❑ An increase in the productivity from 5- to 15-fold over 3GL and waterfall systems development.

❑ Due to the shortened time period, and provision of rapid prototyping, there is an increase in user involvement.

❑ As the system is developed, and is checked against requirements, there is a subsequent reduction in the need for late modification, and post implementation 'maintenance'.

❑ The design approach of each system is standardised on a common agreed pattern.

❑ The end result is a 6-fold reduction in application generation time.

In large corporations there has been a committed move towards the CASE environment. It is no longer a future technology; it is here, and the rewards of adopting it are being obtained. There are, however, several questions that need to be asked before any organisation adopts CASE as their development environment:

❑ Will they be compatible with future SEM?

❑ Is the SEM contained in them appropriate to the needs of analysts?

❑ Is the notation used in the environments a standard, be it notional, national or *de facto?*

The first question has been answered by the discussion in the preceding chapters; there is a need for a more flexible user centred approach to software development. The CASE/IPSE environment goes quite some way to meeting this.

If the CASE environment acts as a vehicle for a variety of software development tools, can they be tailored to fit the way in which the software is developed? Secondly, if there is a flexible view of the software development life cycle within the organisation that is caused by the adoption of CASE then this answers the second question. This means that CASE tools should not try to enforce a particular model on the system's life cycle, i.e. they should allow a set of activities without enforcing an order in the application of the tools. There is still a need, however, to distinguish between those activities that characterise the analysis phase, and those which correspond to the programming phase (the 'front end' and 'back end' respectively).

Table 4.2

The impact of CASE on development

❑ There is an emphasis on the customer requirements and specification of software.

❑ The resulting system – achieved by 'human engineering' - is what the user feels comfortable with.

❑ The system is naturally split into interlocking components which are developed into an application.

❑ There is a reduction in the need for final system testing due to the modules being tested as they are developed.

❑ A system evolves under development rather than being produced.

❑ The roles and responsibilities within the project team are widened and enhanced to cover all aspects of the development process for each individual within the team.

❑ The organisation of the DP department itself will have to alter to one based on the 'development centre' idea, where the department is responsible for the 'core' or 'shell' of the organisation's major systems, and user organisations functional areas are responsible for 'customising'.

❑ The project management has to be done by the team, rather than the manager. Hence the standards of the department will have to alter, along with policies and procedures.

Furthermore, due to the large amount of software that is written in 3GLs there is a need for reverse engineering – the taking of already written software, and generating the design from it. Even if the documentation for existing systems is well written and consistent there will be errors in it. (How much existing documentation is error-free?) Therefore there is a need for reverse engineering within CASE so that the existing software can be maintained within the new environment, or included in new products. The outputs of such reverse engineering can consist of call trees, data descriptions, cross references and flow diagrams for the data within the system.

IPSE goes a stage further than CASE. It supports other 'tools' that provide a wider support environment for the developer, and integrate the individual into the team, and provide the control and management function necessary for the successful completion of large complex projects. It allows project interactions to be controlled, libraries of 'plug-in' modules to be maintained, as well as tailored working methods to be allowed. The extra components, therefore, are administration and management functions [7].

There are several commercial CASE environments on offer; some are linked directly to database products [8]; others are meant as more general development aids [9]; and one offers a complete 'front to back' development environment for a specific machine[10]. This is by no means meant to be a full list of CASE tools!

4GLS – The 'back end'

The CASE environment has a set of 'front end' tools, the analysis and design tools, which were discussed in the previous chapter. It also has a series of 'back end' tools that will aid the developer in the production of code, which is in the form of a high-level computer language, or directly executable programs on a specific target machine. The use of 4GLs in software development has attracted a lot of interest in the computer industry [11]. The 4GL can be used in its own right to develop software, having first done the analysis and design in the traditional manner. However, it is very well suited to the more dynamic approach, i.e. user centred.

Since the use of 4GLs is fairly common the impact of them on development times and reliability of software has been apparent for some length of time. Similarly, the demand for 'good' software increases exponentially along with the amount spent on production and maintenance. It is still significant however, that, as identified in Chapter 1, the percentage of overall effort taken up by the maintenance review modification cycle of released software products is still comparatively large when compared with the actual development time. Therefore, if an SEM is to work successfully it must couple the modern analysis and design tools with 4GLs.

The following table illustrates the significant impact that 4GLs have made on the software development cycle, and specifically it is evident that coupled with modern analysis and design methods they make a powerful and useful complement.

Table 4.3

Impact of 4GLs on development

❑ The effort required in programming and program maintenance can be reduced significantly.

❑ Most applications are design led. The customer's requirements are analysed prior to solution.

❑ Adoption of 4GLs enforces the need for developers to adopt a CASE or IPSE.

❑ Prototyping is required for the true adoption of a 4GL in the development environment.

❑ A significant shift in emphasis is caused by a move away from production of software towards the user being considered as a major partner in development (demand led).

❑ Provision of several 'layered languages' which allow both the professional and the casual user to interact with the 4GL. [8,9,10,11]

Role of the End User

The end user in computing has always been a bone of contention for the more traditional DP departments. As end users become more sophisticated in their requirements and more knowledgeable in their use of computers and information technology in general, then the traditional methods of working will disappear, finally to become redundant. As the business environment becomes more competitive, and local markets can no longer be considered as safe from indigenous suppliers, there is a need to make both management and the knowledge workers more productive. As already stated, automation of the automators needs to be undertaken. To enable this we need to clearly define what we mean by 'knowledge work', and what is required in order to achieve productivity gains.

Knowledge work is that portion of the workload that produces instructions, plans, definitions, report papers and diagnoses, and not administrative and organisational activities. It is closely analogous to the activities of middle and line management, and the work of 'white collar' workers. That does not mean to say, however, that knowledge is not used in the more physical environments, because it is. The more automated the production becomes, the greater the need for a highly skilled workforce, i.e. knowledge work involves thinking about the task in hand, about future tasks and about passing instructions, information and data on in a meaningful way.

The management, administrative, and production tasks that were manual in the past have been aided first by large machines, then mini computers and now by personal computers. The next stage is to link individuals into a whole by the use of communications and sophisticated software that makes adequate use of the technology involved. To enable a further increase in the productivity of the knowledge worker, there has to be made available easily programmed computers. We have this to some extent in the availability of the personal microcomputer and the software that runs on it.

For the DP professional, the explosion in the use of personal computer power has posed considerable problems. These problems usually stem from compatibility, communications and conservation of existing systems and software.

Compatibility of operating systems, software and hardware is necessary to provide adequate support in a corporate environment. Analysis of use shows that apart from the more specialised areas such as engineering workstations and control devices, the majority of people will do most work with just three packages – a spreadsheet, a database and a word processor. Hence the corporate user must be constrained by some form of standardisation of software and hardware.

Table 4.4

End user computing trends

❑ Traditional methods of development are being phased out.

❑ An increase in productivity is required from both the end user and the software developer.

❑ The use of personal computers has generated a mature, sophisticated market for usable software.

❑ Industry-standard operating systems and programming languages are emerging.

❑ Radical change in the support of end users – the move away from the DP department towards an Information Support Centre.

❑ Corporations are becoming leaner and meaner in order to survive.

❑ Software which has a standard core is tailored for different departments/functions in the business.

Communication between the various hardware needs an 'open system' type of strategy. Gone are the days when one manufacturer will be able to tie users to their proprietary systems, despite still trying. Again, the use of LANs (Local Area

Networks) and WANs (Wide Area Networks) needs some form of direction, control and standardisation within the corporate structure. [14,15] Discussion of the selection use and workings of the various networks can be found in the references given.

Conservation is the attitude of some DP departments whereby they remain closed and isolated from the users. If they do this, not only will they fail, but they may also cause the company to fail by not providing effective information.

These problems have caused some of the industry to realise that centralisation of resources is not the answer. The user and developer of software have essentially the same problems, i.e. we need solutions and we need them quickly. Table 4.4 identifies trends in end user computing which must be addressed.

Can any SEM we use take on board these trends and help solve some of the problems created by them? I hope that by now, the arguments presented in the preceding chapters have convinced us to use a more dynamic approach to systems development, and to involve the end user more in this development.

The Role of the Information Centre

If we move away from traditional DP, what model can we use to provide adequate support and service to users? There will still be a need for technical support for most users. This is because computing power should be seen as a business tool, and not a specialist experiment, in much the same way that people can use a telephone or a car, but do not know how either work. That is the work of the specialist.

Also the more sophisticated the users become, the more they will require support of a specialised nature. Therefore, we should attempt to provide support, development, advice and initial training within the organisation.

The symptoms for the requirement for an information centre are precisely those that are the cause of the software crisis mentioned earlier – missed software development deadlines, crisis help, and fighting fires rather than planned action, long delays in the preparation of simple reports for management and myriad complaints and frustration from users regarding the DP department.

As in all developments, the justification for the evolution of an information centre must be based on a cost\benefit analysis. However, serious thought should be given to user satisfaction as a tangible benefit. The changes in attitude and ability will not happen immediately – as with all things these take time, but they should be seen as increases in productivity and enthusiasm in end users.

Diversification of service to end user departments is a necessity in the business environment as it becomes more complex and more automated.

Table 4.5

Aims of the Information Centre

❑ Support of the end user throughout the period of development of systems.

❑ Training of new and existing users in the use of existing and developing systems.

❑ Development of applications with end users as effectively and efficiently as possible.

❑ To ensure that departmental information applications and systems are consistent throughout the organisation, i.e. information is seen as a corporate resource and is shared.

❑ Hardware and software is standardised throughout departments.

❑ To provide an evaluation and development/tailoring faculty to users.

❑ To keep control over the accuracy and integrity of the main corporate information database.

❑ To ensure that the systems that are used have the required security and audit facilities built into them.

❑ To ensure that any relevant legislation is obeyed when developing solutions or systems.

❑ Provision of advice, news, tips and hints to the user population as a whole.

❑ Formation of corporate information strategy in conjunction with business strategy.

To provide sufficient resources and enable enough development to be done in an environment where end users are more sophisticated in their requirements, while still naive in their understanding of ancillary problems involved in the production of robust systems, creates considerable headaches for the developer using a traditional SEM. Walls instead of bridges tend to be built by the DP department in order to keep the end user away.

The dynamic SEM can be used as a bridge, thus encouraging the users of systems to be fully integrated into the development process. Initially, this may appear to cost more as the development enters the first phase of requirement analysis, but by using automated generation or prototyping to flesh out the requirements, and fully generated code which entirely maps those requirements, the costs associated with maintenance and 'bug-shooting' will be reduced, and – hpefully – almost entirely limited to simple corrections in the system.

Acceleration of Life Cycles

To enable an organisation to maintain its position, it needs a rapid cycle of development. As the business environment speeds up and becomes more complex, information becomes the fuel that the business needs to operate on. We need to know the following:

❑ The current position

❑ Why we wish to change or alter the situation

❑ What can be done to change the situation

❑ What it is possible for us to do

❑ A plan for moving from where we are now to where we want to be

❑ An evaluation. (Did we do it?)

Table 4.6

Characteristics of Accelerating Life Cycles

❑ Adoption of high productivity software development methods.

❑ Development times for systems need to be compressed from an average of 18 months to 4 months.

❑ Low-cost and easily available standard hardware and software modules.

❑ Automated support for functions that were done manually, or not at all (e.g. test nets, and program documentation).

This sounds very similar to the system life cycle, and indeed it is. The trouble is that the life cycle in business is contracting. Does the current system development method you are using take this into account? To accelerate the system life cycle, we need to take on board as a matter of urgency that a lack of personal productivity amongst information systems developers and management has resulted in the formation of bottlenecks in the office where there are still either manual systems or insufficiently efficient automated ones. These inefficiencies cause management problems and keep them from the consideration of important actions. This reinforces the slow down in personal productivity. If this situation is left for too long, the organisation locks up and fails to function properly, eventually destroying itself.

What are the characteristics that need to be coped with in our SEM?

Existing computer systems need to be re-evaluated to fit in with the environment as already outlined earlier. Integrated, personalised, modernised and restructured software is essential.

We can make significant increases in our own productivity by using modern development methods. After the initial requirement phase we can adopt certain software generation regimes that give us consistent designs and flexible as well as reliable software. We have discussed the front end environment needed for software production and development, but so far we have not considered the 'back end' or code generation from our design. The subsequent section of this chapter introduces the use of code generation techniques on two common functions in software. Firstly that of input screens used for basic data input and report structures. The third common feature is the data handling facility, and the fourth the actual control structure of the program or system – we can 'paint' screens, determine the report layout, and decide on the file structure, by using some of the proprietary data handling packages that are available. However converting them to stand-alone programs is a further step that has only been considered by a few of the vendors of such packages. Some 4GLs need further action on the part of developers to satisfy the user adequately – i.e., to provide a solution that is 80% acceptable.

Generation of Screens, Reports and Programs

As was seen in the example in the last chapter, the extraction of information from the client file is a significant part of the program, as well as the maintenance of the data contained within the file. The outline structure of the program was developed, and suggestions made as to the appearance of screens and reports. The next step in our design process is to generate the set of screens required and the basic reports that go to make up the core of the system. This can be done directly using the 'screen/report painters' in the CASE environments or, if not available, on standard report and screen layout documents. (Several commercial products allow the construction of elaborate applications in a simple and consistent manner. These applications are built by defining and specifying the data, screens, reports and control menus interactively.)

The output from the screen generation consists of details regarding the position and type of field allocated to the screen, as well as its length. Also, the file or database in which the field is stored is given, along with the screen number (a screen can consist of many pages). The second part of the figure is a pictorial representation of the output as it appears on the screen. Additional fields, such as the date and time, are obtained directly from the system. Each of the screens that are required by the system can be generated in the same way, and shown to the user. Indeed, some systems would allow the developer, and the customer, to try out the screen before finalising the format [12]. The next step is to generate the code from the screen design if this is desired. To illustrate this, here is a program generated from a screen design program [13]. The final code happens to be C, but other target languages and machine types are available from suppliers, and third parties. Many of these are available both on the PC and on mini, and mainframe environments, and the selection of which to use is beyond the scope of this book. Needless to say, if we wish to increase productivity, then there is a need to use some form of automatic generation of code.

Field definitions for screen : CLIENT

Page	Row	Col	Data Store	Field	Type	Width	Dec*
1	9	48	CLIENT	TELEPHONE	Character	14	
1	11	48	CLIENT	CONSULTANT	Character	20	
1	5	27	CLIENT	NAME1	Character	20	
1	6	27	CLIENT	NAME2	Character	20	
1	5	60	CLIENT	TITLE	Character	4	
1	9	12	CLIENT	ADDRESS1	Character	20	
1	10	12	CLIENT	ADDRESS2	Character	20	
1	11	12	CLIENT	ADDRESS3	Character	20	
1	13	12	CLIENT	POSTCODE	Character	8	
1	3	27	CLIENT	JOBNUMBER	Character	10	

Content of page : 1

```
SCR 1          HOUSE PURCHASE SYSTEM          Date : DDMMYY
                                              Time : HH:MM:SS
Job Number     XXXXXXXXXX

Client's First Name XXXXXXXXXXXXXXXXXXXX   Title     XXXX
        Second Name   XXXXXXXXXXXXXXXXXXXX

Address             XXXXXXXXXXXXXXXXXXXX   Telephone XXXXX
                    XXXXXXXXXXXXXXXXXXXX
                    XXXXXXXXXXXXXXXXXXXX   Consultant  XXXXX
Postcode            XXXXXXXX
```

*Dec=decimal places

Figure 4.2 Output from a typical screen generator program

The screen definition given in Figure 4.2 is converted to the relevant C code, as in Figure 4.3a. The text of the screen is given between the quotes, and its position as the numbers in the next field. The field attributes are given in Figure 4.3b (the screen colour, field type, and any validation functions required). The field characteristics are read from the data dictionary of the project, and transferred accordingly to the screen definition, thus allowing the automatic generation of the code. The respective parts of the screen definition are inserted into a skeleton program which handles screen requests, and interfaces with the database, or program files.

```
BURSTREC clnttxt[] = {
    "SCR 1",0x100,0x7,
    "HOUSE PURCHASE SYSTEM",0x1a00,0x7,
    "Date :",0x3c00,0x7,
    "Jobnumber",0x303,0x7,
    "Clients First Name",0x305,0x7,
    "Title",0x3805,0x7,
    "Second Name",0xb06,0x7,
    "Address",0x209,0x7,
    "Telephone",0x2809,0x7,
    "Consultant",0x280b,0x7,
    "Postcode",0x20d,0x7,
    NULL
    };
```

Figure 4.3a The screen definition with position of text

```
int clnt_cs_2[]  = {0x0,0x3ff,0xfffe,0x7ff,0x0,0x0};
int clnt_cs_3[]  = {0x0,0x0,0xfffe,0x7ff,0xfffe,0x7ff};
int clnt_cs_4[]  = {0x0,0x0,0xfffe,0x7ff,0xfffe,0x7ff};
int clnt_cs_5[]  = {0x0,0x0,0xfffe,0x7ff,0xfffe,0x7ff};
int clnt_cs_6[]  = {0x0,0x3ff,0xfffe,0x7ff,0xfffe,0x7ff};
int clnt_cs_7[]  = {0x1300,0x3ff,0x0,0x0,0x2a,0x9};
int clnt_cs_8[]  = {0x0,0x0,0xfffe,0x7ff,0xfffe,0x7ff};
int clnt_cs_9[]  = {0x0,0x0,0xfffe,0x7ff,0xfffe,0x7ff};
int clnt_cs_10[] = {0x400,0x0,0xfffe,0x7ff,0xfffe,0x7ff};
int clnt_cs_11[] = {0x0,0x3ff,0xfffe,0x7ff,0x0,0x0};
```

Figure 4.3b Definition of the data fields

The only coding the programmer has to perform are the special validation functions, which are part of the field definitions (Figure 4.3d). Hence, by using the screen painter for menus and individual input and enquiry screens it only remains to generate the reports necessary for the project; which can also be done in a similar manner.

Again from considering the report program structure given in the previous chapter, the program or module which generates the report can be based on a similar set of language statements, e.g. a report is paged, it has a heading on each page, with possibly a page number and date. It will have a sub-heading on top of the page consisting of field descriptions corresponding to the columns of the report, and finally a set of lines on which are the selected data fields from the database or files used by the system. In addition to the standard structure there may also be some form of final line consisting of total values or messages. See Figure 4.4.

The code can be generated from the above definitions in a way similar to the screens, so that the generation of the bulk of the programs within the system becomes

```
typedef struct {
    char jobnumber[10];
    char cname1[20];
    char title[4];
    char cname2[20];
    char address1[20];
    char telephone[14];
    char address2[20];
    char address3[20];
    char consultant[20];
    char postcode[9];
    } CLNTTYPE;
```

Figure 4.3c Definition of the data record

```
FIELDSPEC clnt_fields[] = {
    11,0xf03,0x342,0xa,clnt_cs_2,valjob,
    131,0x1805,0x302,0x14,clnt_cs_3,NULL,
    535,0x3f05,0x302,0x4,clnt_cs_4,valtitle,
    571,0x1806,0x302,0x14,clnt_cs_5,NULL,
    991,0xb09,0x302,0x14,clnt_cs_6,NULL,
    1405,0x3809,0x302,0xe,clnt_cs_7,NULL,
    1621,0xb0a,0x302,0x14,clnt_cs_8,NULL,
    2041,0xb0b,0x302,0x14,clnt_cs_9,NULL,
    2461,0x380b,0x342,0x14,clnt_cs_10,NULL,
    2860,0xb0d,0x142,0x8,clnt_cs_11,NULL
    };
RECSPEC clnt_rec = {
    clnt_fields,
    10
    };
```

Figure 4.3d Field specifications for data type, and validation

automatic. The screens and reports generated can be controlled via programs or menus, again generated in the same way. The whole project is dynamically modifiable, and hence suitable for customer involvement and prototyping.

```
Client Short List  HOUSE PURCHASE SYSTEM  Date: DD/MM/YY

Client's second name    First name    JobNo    Consultant

XXXXXXXXXXXXXXX         XXXXXXXXXXX   XXXXXXX  XXXXXXXXX

          Report width        80      Columns

          Report page Length 60       Lines

          Page Header Length 5        Lines

          Report Lines Per Page55     Lines

Field Definition for Client Short List   CLNTLST

Column        File      Field        Type        Width

    2         CLIENT    CNAME2       Character    20
   24         CLIENT    CNAME1       Character    20
   46         CLIENT    JOBNUMBER    Character    10
   58         CLIENT    CONSULTANT   Character    20
```

Figure 4.4 Example report Structure/Layout

Summary

The environment for the programmer and the analyst described in the last two chapters can be provided by the adoption of CASE or IPSE. However, even if it is not possible to obtain these products, the developer can use some of the tools described to aid in software development. It is possible to perform the requirements analysis using a suitable analysis methodology, design the programs, then code the program in a suitable language. This method is closely analogous to the traditional approach, and will therefore take longer than taking advantage of modern environments. The object of any SEM is to improve user confidence in the product, and the confidence of the project team in what it is producing. The overall effect is to base the implementation on engineered user requirements. The strategy for software production is summarised in Figure 4.5.

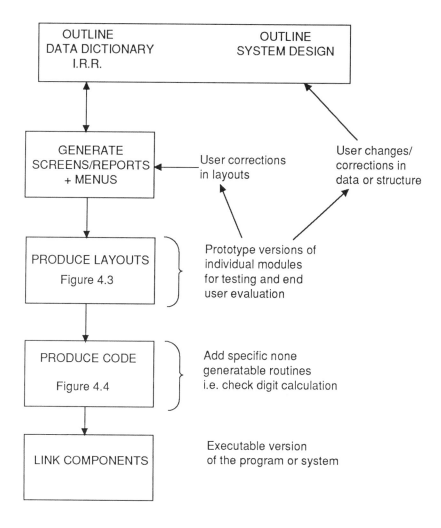

Figure 4.5 Strategy for production of software

Exercises

1) Using the outline definition of the information required in the House Purchasing System given in Chapter 2, either by using a 'screen painter', or a screen definition program, generate a set of suitable screens for the menus required.

2) Try to implement the menu structure by using a suitable high-level language, or a proprietary software package.

3) Draw out the structure of a report which contains details of students – the student's name, course, department and examination entered.

References

[1] Learmouth and Burchett Managements Systems Plc, Systems Design Methodology Course.

[2] P. Clare and I. Coe, Structured Systems Analysis and Design Methodology, Prentice-Hall, 1988.

[3] Yourden and Constantine, Structured Design, Prentice-Hall, 1978.

[4] C.Gane and T.Sarson, Structured Systems Analysis, IST.

[5] M. Jackson, System Development, Prentice-Hall 1983.

[6] S.M. Deen, Fundamentals of Data Base Systems, MacMillan, 1977.

[7] Eighteen Months of Alvey Software Engineering, Alvey news article, published by the ALVEY Directorate.

[8] ORACLE CASE technology, Oracle Corp UK Ltd.

[9] Excelerator, Excelerator Software Products.

[10] Corvision, Cortex Ltd.

[11] K Grindley, The Grindley report, IDPM, 21 Russell St. London WC2 B5UB.

[13] D. Benyon and S. Skidmore, Towards a toolkit for the Systems Analyst, The Computer Journal, VOL 30, No1, 1987.

[14] Tanenbaum, Computer Networks, Prentice-Hall.

[15] M. Purser, Computers and Telecommunications Networks, Blackwell.

5

The Man Machine Interface

Objectives

Improvement of the design and prototype by examining the overall behaviour of the system in relation to the user.

Improvement of the user interface.

Identification of what a good MMI is, and what characteristics it might display.

Requirements for a Human Interface

For a considerable time it has been well known that a good interface between man and machine helps to make a good piece of software. However, the interface between the human being and the software is complex and can be sophisticated [1,2].

What makes a good interface for one particular user may not be suitable for another. The whole area of Man Machine Interface (MMI) covers diverse topics and disciplines, from psychology to screen definition [3]. It is not just the consideration of how the screen and reports look, but involves a deeper understanding of the requirements of a good MMI.

These requirements are currently split between six research themes, and are included in MMI research:

❏ The organisational philosophy and strategic requirements

❏ Maintenance and refurbishment of current systems

❏ SEM and the design of software

❏ Machine Hardware, and interaction methods

❏ User role in the design, development and implementation of systems

❏ Cognitive ability and requirements of the user.

These areas are aimed at introducing some modern developments into the design methods, such as expert systems, natural language processing, vision, and voice activated response, as well as improvement in the use and presentation of current systems.

The ALVEY project on the other hand identified two areas worth consideration in the enhancement of MMI:

❏ Pattern analysis, which logically splits into two, image processing and speech processing

❏ Display of information, and the technology that is used in displays.

Hence the area called MMI covers a large part of design considerations, and has great importance to the designer in the adoption of a suitable design philosophy, as well as an influence on the finished product, in terms of both software and hardware.

Design and Development Methods

If we consider the MMI as a serious part of the design effort the accommodation of MMI in the design process requires some thought and effort on the part of the designer. The requirements of a good MMI need to be understood if users are to be provided with a piece of software that fully meets their requirements. The design requirements that are affected directly by an enhanced MMI are, of course precisely

Table 5.1

Design and Development of an MMI

❏ The inclusion of end user considerations and wishes in the software design process.

❏ A consideration of human factors that are to be included in any MMI within the system.

❏ Modifications and enhancements to the design and development methods, to include MMI and human factors.

❏ Examination of possible machine architectures, both hardware and software support for systems.

❏ Adoption of design techniques which allow good MMI.

those topics we have covered earlier. Table 5.1 provides a summary of what we should consider important in our SEM.

By adoption of the 'development' rather than the 'production' mentality in DP departments and software houses, most of the factors mentioned will be catered for in our SEM. Hence we should be able to obtain a good MMI. The user must, therefore, be considered as an equal partner in the development process, and has the chance to influence the design and development of the system.

A consideration of the MMI should be found throughout the development process either by using and criticising a prototype, or included throughout the design process as a prerequisite of how the system should behave and appear to the users.

Human Factors

So far our discussion of SEMs has included the user in a semi formal way. In the development and design of systems which are an integral part of clerical and office procedure the role of the user takes on further significance. Indeed most SEMs concentrate on the attempt to automate the clerical process without consideration of the end user. The systems developed from a limited set of tools, or those systems which have been developed without close consideration of the end user, can be viewed as exclusively concerned with the work place, i.e. the organisation and ergonomics of a task. (How the system is used, and the more technical aspects of the procedure computerised). Even the human interface is probably considered in a similar manner [4]).

We will also probably be able to recognise an 'inhuman' system when we see one! A badly designed system can vary from a simple bad screen layout which does not show all the necessary data, to a hazardous system. Even the more common ergonomic factors, such as keyboard and screen type may not be taken into account when designing a system. The more common elements of ergonomics can be catered for when considering the hardware, and final implementation of the system:

❏ VDU flicker and glare as well as colour and size

❏ Lighting inadequacy and placement

❏ Seating arrangement; the height of desks and chairs.

All the above mechanical ergonomic issues can be solved, but will probably remain a problem through lack of consideration or money during the implementation phase.

Organisational ergonomics consists of the following areas: social contact, environment, and job content and purpose. Most of our current systems do not make any allowance for the factors stated. They leave out one significant characteristic of an organisation, and that is that the humans in the organisation are on the whole a social animal. Therefore, when we design an MMI we invariably concentrate on the mechanistic aspects of the screen, report and menu, sometimes adding type of equipment. In most studies of work and factors which go to make up that elusive thing 'job satisfaction' the factor that is given most prominence among clerical workers is social contact [6]. Most organisational developments and alterations are concerned with improvement in communication both horizontally across , and vertically down the organisational structure, without due regard to the existing human mechanisms that exist in the structure.

Secondly, when we automate a task the people who operate the system are monitoring and controlling the task, but are no longer in symbiosis. The task of control takes over, and hence automation makes the original task remote from the user. The danger of this approach is that there is no specific knowledge of the 'product' and physical contact with the process itself is reduced, hence reducing job satisfaction and identification with the product. There can be a great advantage in simulation of end systems for potential users (e.g.flight simulators) which give the user the look and feel of the real process. The operators knowledge and process awareness is often lost at the design stage because we do not consider it in the design. This leads to a 'closing down' or specialisation of job content, so that it becomes preplanned or programmed, and the monitoring of operator performance is done continuously, or at pre-fixed intervals. The design of automated processes has already hit the factory floor, and is coming into offices. Despite the implied criticism above, most people will welcome a new system if it is needed and fairly well designed. However, there is usually some user resistance to most systems, and it would be better if the acceptance of a new system was easier to accomplish. To do this, a system designer must understand the organisational context in which the system is to be used, and adapt the method by which the design is reached to include 'human factors'.

The Inclusion of Human Factors and Methods

The inadequacy of some of the current design and analysis methods is illustrated by the way they do not handle what is essentially one of the main purposes for computerisation or automation of a problem. The interaction of the human with the machine is of primary importance, when one is designing systems that are to take the place of office or commercial areas of work, which have previously been dealt with by humans, or only partly computerised. Existing methodologies can be characterised by how they deal with the following factors:

❏ The narrowing of job content, and the mechanistic production-led development

❏ The development of formal lines of communication within the organisation

❏ The belief that technology is neutral in its interaction with both the social and organisational context.

To some extent the first item on the list can be dealt with by adopting a more flexible and user centred approach to system development, and ultimately to the SEM we use. The second area of contention is coupled with the often complex interactions that exist in an organisation, and take the form of 'communications' both official and unofficial. There is information loss in any form of electronic means of communication, or indeed any form of communication that is impersonal. The subtleties of human communication are not matched by electronic means, e.g. there is a difference between the printed page, and the same information as presented on a screen [6].

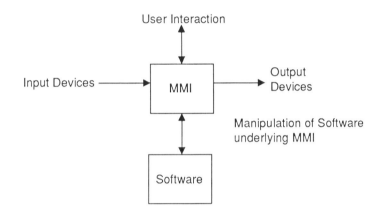

Figure 5.1 MMI and Software

Thirdly, the use of technology to monitor employees, while understandable in the context of the drive for efficiency and productivity, can be very disruptive and detrimental to the user acceptance of a system. Even when not designed as a fundamental part of a system, it can be used for monitoring purposes in both a conscious and unconscious fashion. In any case, whether we like it or not, the technology we develop can no longer be assumed to be neutral in its effect on the workplace. The controlling mechanisms we can establish belong to the following categories:

❏ Limitation of the discretion of developers and designers of the system, so as to embed covert controls into the system

❏ High dependence and integration of the team approach into work, without the collective responsibility and satisfaction

❏ The use of checklists, rules and procedures without explanation

❏ The production and monitoring of detailed plans, goals and performance without adequate feedback.

Compare the list given above with the aims of some of the system methodologies such as SSADM, Yourden and so on. There is a similarity with the aims of the methods, and the list. This is not to say that the main aim of the methods is to apply covert control as a direct consequence of using the method. The need for the inclusion of control aims in any methodology is to provide a feedback mechanism to project management, and give the project team a set of milestones at which 'deliverables' are to be produced. However, when the main controlling influence is the user rather than the project management then the mechanisms by which the project is controlled are tied up essentially in user requirements, and the 'human factors' of the control and communication system embedded in the project.

Table 5.2

Additional MMI Factors influencing SEM

Presentation: The design of information layout such as colours, size and definition as well as user interaction, must be considered at an early stage.

Methods: Inclusive in the adoption of a suitable SEM consideration must be given the cognitive level of the person using the system – the same information presented to a technical person may be inappropriate for a shop floor worker. The analysis of tasks that have to be done as a direct consequence of manipulation of the system by various people who have differing requirements must be undertaken. (In the past this has been relegated to the operations manual, or to a description of the screens available on the system).

Functions: Since the human interface changes the requirements and the performance, as well as the appearance and feel of the system, then that fully developed system must be adaptive to the levels of differing user interaction.

Organisation of user/production team: A lot of systems developed are used by a single person only. However a lot of the development is done by a team. If the team is responsible from start to finish of a project then the area of potential conflict is reduced to a manageable proportion.

Ability of user: Applications are becoming complex, but the user is no longer an expert, hence the need for software that has an easy-to-use interface. Witness the development of 'windowing', 'icons' and on-line help facilities and user support.

Methods and Tools

The preceding chapters introduced and developed a methodology which can be used to dynamically introduce user requirements and direct involvement in the design of the system. The overall aim was to produce a service to clients which provides them with a piece of usable software.

There are, however, some further considerations which are a direct influence on the production of software. These are based on how the developer approaches the actual development, rather than how the development proceeds.

The organisational context of the development should not be overlooked; it should be modified to include the creation of project teams on specific targets. These teams should have direct responsibility to proceed with the software development from start to finish as well as being given direct access to the user. Similarly, the external components of the DP department or of an organisation need to be adapted to include local or accessible expertise, so that the DP department as such disappears and a 'development centre' takes over much of its functions, in conjunction with user departments (if resources permit).

In the case of a software house, it should provide good advice and a back-up service to users, which includes such things as 'hot-lines' and on site training and support, as well as effective manuals for the products. The effect of this is to decentralise software production. The more peripheral operations of a DP department are fed to the user departments, leaving the actual development of the core systems to the centre. In the event of any difficulty arising the user departments can ask for advice and assistance from the development centre.

Information Presentation, Functionality and User Ability

The way the system presents information to the user is dependent on the technical design factors of the hardware and software that make the system and the user's cognitive set of abilities, Figure 5.2 overleaf. The overall aim is to improve the system quality and its usability, the impressions of which may not be the same for all users of the system. [7,8]

Since the usability of the system is so dependent on the cognitive set of the user, as well as the initial design requirements, why, then, do we ignore the user from our considerations?

Secondly, why are the requirements of a design not produced to an exacting standard, or why are they not discussed with the user?

Consider the following, which is taken from a specification given to me some years ago:

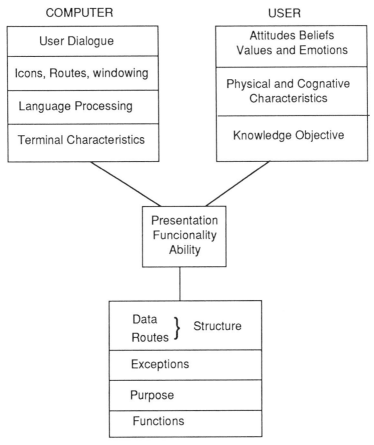

Figure 5.2 The Computer User System Interface

1. Develop an input screen to allow customer records to be input.

2. Develop an input screen that allows the following transactions to be performed on a customer file indexed on customer number: Add, Change, Delete.

   The screen should have a standard background, the message prompts shall be in normal foreground, and the data entry fields shall be highlighted. Error messages caused by incorrect input shall appear at the bottom of the screen in row 23.

The second specification is much tighter, and can be discussed in detail with the user in either the form of a layout chart or in the form of a prototyped screen. Specification 1 may have resulted in a screen similar to the one as produced by 2, but there will probably have been a lot of discussion with the user. In either case, it illustrates the necessity of user involvement at an early stage in the development. The attitudes, beliefs and preferences of the user can best be expressed in a discussion with the system designer which is based around a suitable model or prototype of the proposed system. In addition the design of the interface can be adapted to take into consideration these views.

However, the more complex the system the more flexible and accommodating the user interface must become. As a simple example consider a first time user and an expert user of the same system (a word processor, for example); the expert may know by heart most of the commands to drive the system, but the first time user will probably rely heavily on the manual and any on-line help facilities available. In fact, there has been considerable interest shown in personalised or adaptive interfaces for different users. This is where the user's preferences and idiosyncrasies can be stored by the system, so that it adapts to the particular user. To some extent we can see this trend in various microcomputer products that are on the market. These usually have some sort of 'macro', or keypress recording facility that allows preset and commonly used key strokes to be stored. Also commonly provided with these products is an on-line help facility which is context sensitive.

Often this concept of usability is alien to the software developer, since all measurements of usefulness are against initial user requirements [7,8]. There have been some attempts at actually measuring the usability of products which are fully developed, and are based on initial user requirements which will probably have changed in the development period. See Table 5.3, below.

Table 5.3

Measurements of Usability

Functions, tasks and paths:
Split the system into the relevant functions and mechanisms for achieving those functions; similarly the tasks needed to accomplish those functions from the user. After which identify the control paths via which the user 'navigates' the system.

Enumeration of results:
This is a quantitative analysis of factors relating to system performance. A full set of measurement criteria are given in [9].

Evaluation:
Monitoring the use of the system, following the identified tasks and paths used. Questioning users of the system as to their subjective feelings as regard to performance, accuracy, helpfulness and availability. Ask also for specific examples of good and bad behaviour.

Architecture

The consideration of the influence of emerging and available technologies on the design strategy of systems, and the resulting alteration of the user's perception on the finished product, is often overlooked. Part of the 'drive' towards MMI has been the manipulability of the system in terms of the human interaction it allows via input, output and display devices. As these improve they enable a facilitation of interaction that is costly in terms of hardware requirements as well as design of the software driving it. However, products have emerged that are designed to give a good MMI on the cheaper and smaller micros that are sold in the High Street. A typical example is the 'mouse' driven software bundled into the price of certain machines, along with windows and presentation packages. See Table 5.4.

Coupled with the impact of hardware sophistication has been the study of how the end user interacts with the system. The increase in capability of the average user as familiarity is gained with the software (the Learning Curve) must also be taken into account.

At this point it may be worthwhile to find what is currently available to the designer and developer in regard to 'software tools' as well as technical specifications of hardware. Almost any of the trade journals will carry accounts of new software and hardware.

Table 5.4

Architectural considerations

Decentralisation:
Distribution of computer power enables group working and co-operation via individuals and departments.

Interaction:
That between the user and the machine has improved with the availability of bit mapped displays, clear graphics, mice, touch pads and such like.

Expertise:
There has been an improvement in the ability of software houses to cope with these new methods of interaction, and adapt them for their own products.

Standards:
The 'user interface' has become semi-standard across a variety of products; these have then become 'de facto' standards.

Prototyping and the MMI

Relationships between the decisions taken during the design process, can be identified as follows (starting from early to late in the development, and following through sequentially):

1) Fundamental characteristics of the system, such as response, information presentation, transactions, tasks, and organisational information.

2) Dialogue and user tasks, help facilities and screen/report design, procedures and user feedback.

3) Implementation and user training and support.

N.B. The choice of hardware can also be made in stage 1. This may not be a specific designated machine, but could be generic, such as a micro, a network or a centralised/decentralised system.

At each stage the user can evaluate the development of the system, and provide the required feedback to the development team. The prototype or system simulation then becomes a vehicle on which the project is based. See Chapter 2 for a more detailed discussion on prototyping. The improvement in the MMI should be significant, since the end user is involved.

Mice, Menus and the User

So far in this chapter I have introduced some ideas and factors governing the adoption of standard MMIs, but are there any existing MMIs which can be used to advantage for the basis of any design which we may propose. Obviously there will be a considerable difference in the applications we intend for internal use, and those which will be released, or put on sale. There are perhaps various levels at which we can address this, and possibly attack the problem of a 'sufficient MMI'.

Broadly speaking the user interfaces with both the machine operating system, its mechanical components and the application package in use. Each application package will be controlled by a different set of parameters, which will cause the application to perform a set of given tasks in a specific order. However there has been in recent years a set of so called 'industry standard' products which have been sold to the public, and commercial DP. These 'de facto' standards can be adopted to our advantage, and to the advantage of the users. Most corporate solutions have in the essence some form of standardisation for both hardware and software usage.

The usual types of software found on corporate PCs are a database of some sort, a word processor and a spreadsheet. These may exist in the form of an integrated package, but the principal is the same. For the larger corporate machine there may be some diversity in the 'look and feel' of application software written for it from differing vendors, or by in house teams. The typical user can be insulated from this diversity by careful selection of software and hardware.

Therefore, the user interface must come to terms with some of the diversity offered, and provide a consistent gateway for users, be they novices or experts. Again in the personal computer field the typical user does not exist. There are two broad categories: the first insists on doing everything possible via the operating system, the second has adopted some form of interface. They probably both have a requirement for the same application package. The package must therefore be capable of operation in both environments i.e. directly from the operating system cursor, and subservient to the interface. The former type of user tends to be the developer and implementor, and the latter the actual user.

We can identify some trends in software suppliers' offerings. If these become widespread then they may give us some ideas on our own developments.

Table 5.5

Trends in MMI

❏ WISIWYG displays (what you see is what you get!) obvious maybe, but let the user preview and confirm that's the result they want

❏ To achieve quality interfaces we need high-resolution bit-mapped screens, and the ability to manipulate work objects directly on it

❏ Objects are selected, manipulated and acted upon by selecting the action we wish to perform

❏ Standardisation of menus and facilities offered by packages;Ease of use either directly via the keyboard, or by mouse and or tablet

❏ Visual appeal and impact

❏ Attempt to provide the same facilities' look and feel across a variety of hardware platforms

❏ A standard set of tools, libraries and facilities to help build applications which look and perform in a similar manner.

These are fine as far as the average user needs are known, but what advantages do they offer over traditional systems each with diverse user interfaces and control methods interacting with the hardware?

Firstly they save time because if the applications run on any machine, and all have a standard set of interfaces, then the user has a lower learning curve, and the developer knows what the user interface has to do.

Secondly they should allow the use of a variety of input methods, and be configurable to suit individual needs and requirements.

Thirdly by using standard building blocks the developer can produce more consistent applications in a shorter time.

Lastly applications written to perform under a particular MMI have to have additional features so as to fully utilise the environment, thus effectively making the applications more powerful.

The learning curve is important, and individual application knowledge can often be used to learn the next application interface. Despite this the first MMI met by users may be difficult for them to understand, and use, so that they cannot perform significant tasks on the application package. Therefore, examples, on-line help and tutorials may play a part in the overall product.

There are some difficulties that are caused by the adoption of the MMI. With the increase in power of applications it has become almost impractical to drive them from the operating command line directly. Many machines only have character-based screens, and application packages should operate in an identical fashion for bit-mapped screens. Due to the overheads imposed by the interface such programs tend to monopolise the CPU so that the slower machines tend to display a disjointed performance.

A cynic may say that it is just an excuse to make us adopt the 20/33Mhz processor as standard. Fortunately the relative price for all this power is dropping, but there are a lot of users out there who are perfectly happy using one or two standard software packages on older machines, and will continue to do so. This means that the standard MMI is a long way off, and that it is only important in the corporate environment where support of diverse products is difficult. There is also the resistance to standardisation, if you haven't met it you soon will. We should be able to overcome this by education, persuasion and example. Graphical user interfaces cut across all machine types, they have a variety of dedicated users, and are not restricted to the hairy arty types using desktop publishing, but are a sophisticated tool that we should consider in any of our developments.

Summary

The availability of advanced hardware at a reasonable cost has allowed the spread of computer power throughout the organisation. There has been a lag between availability of the power and its use by equally sophisticated software. The average user is now aware of the potential of these machines, and expects software that is sufficiently adaptable. The manipulation of software is also dependent on the type of corporate users; they no longer wish to know how to operate a machine, they just require results. This imposes on the designer an extra task of providing an interface mechanism which will allow the various users of software to get those results, be they beginners or relative experts. Hence considerations of what a good MMI is should be included in any SEM we care to adopt.

Exercises

1) Implement the houseplan/purchase screens using a suitable method, and try to change the presentation by suitable use of colour (if available), highlighting, and messages on user input error.

2) Consider two input methods:

a) An on-line order entry system, which allows orders to be accepted over the phone.

b) A traditional method of entry, such as document processing, keying, error reporting, and then processing.

Design the screens and the documents in either case, and then specify the error messages and handling capabilities of each system.

3) Which method of input given above will meet the most criteria given for what is a 'good' MMI, and which one would involve the user in more system manipulation?

References

[1] T. Palmer, Software Design and the User Interface, Systems International, March 1987.

[2] E. Edmund, Man Machine Interface, Conference on Interdisciplinary Information Technology, Bradford April 88.

[3] ALVEY Directorate, Man Machine Interface Strategy, August 84.

[4] N. Bjorn-Anderson, Are "Human Factors" Human?, The Computer Journal, Vol 31, No 5, 1988, pp 386-390.

[5] N. Bjorn-Anderson et al, The Impact of Systems Change in Organisations, Sijthoff and Noordhoff, Amsterdam 1979.

[6] Dillon et al, Reading from paper versus reading from Screen, The Computer Journal, Vol 31, No 5, 1988, pp 457-456.

[7] A. P. Jagodjinski and D. D. Clarke, A multidimensional Approach to the Measurement of Human Computer Performance, The Computer Journal, Vol 31, No 5, 1988, pp 409-419.

[8] D. A. Tyldesley, Employing Usability Engineering in the Development of Office Products, The Computer Journal, Vol 31, No 5, 1988, pp 431-436.

[9] J. Whiteside et al, Handbook of Human-Computer Interaction, ed M. Helander, North Holland Publishers, 1988.

6

Software Quality

Objectives

Achieving reliability in the software design.

Identification of 'software quality'

Methods of measuring reliability and quality.

Specifications: Formal or otherwise

Quality Requirements

Quality software is obtained by considering a set of factors, which interact with each other, and which must be designed into the system at an early enough stage so as to influence the end product, and therefore contribute to its reliability. Measurement of said software quality is perhaps difficult to perform; on one hand it can be made into quantitative evaluation of programs and code complexity [1], and on the other merely measured subjectively. The program code complexity can be compared with problem complexity if the problem has been faithfully encoded. (There are probably several correct algorithms for every problem, some of which will have different complexity measurements.)

As an example consider a program that processes a file sequentially and generates a total value for just one of its fields. Now compare that program with another that performs the cross product multiplication of two matrices. The former has a lower complexity measure. Also, we could probably rewrite both of these programs in several different target languages, and again the measures of complexity should be similar for each category, but my programs should look different to yours. This has led to the development of a set of measurements based on 'style' of programming[2].

Witness also the increase in the adoption of structured programming techniques and languages that allow the full exploitation of these development methods. As the automation of the programming task increases we should see solutions to problems that consist of well structured blocks of code which have known complexity and are correct. However, there will still be a need to tailor end results, and to develop solutions to the more complex problems that are not soluble by use of 4GLs or application generators. So, there will still be a need for these products to be tested as we develop them [3]. Lastly, there is a further area which will expand rapidly, namely the formal specification and validation of software. These methods should provide products that not only meet specifications, but which can also be proved to be mathematically correct [4,5]. Table 6.1 identifies quality factors.

Table 6.1

Factors of Software Quality

Reliability: The software or system performs those functions that are required of it. It can also be seen as a process of error elimination and their removal by design and modification, so that software meets the original requirements.

Efficiency: The software produces the required information in a timely and accurate manner.

Usability: The software is produced with a sufficient MMI, and therefore causes the user no surprises during operation.

Security: The software produced does not allow the user to inadvertently destroy its working data. Included in it are the usual procedures for detection of unauthorised access, as well as the ability to take copies and backups of data.

Modifiability: If we have used a good SEM, then by definition the software can be altered to cope with the usual changes in the user requirements, and the changes in organisation.

Reusability: Often the code produced and developed for one system can be applied to others with little or no modification.

Design Metrics

The idea of 'metrics' is to quantify some of the properties discussed earlier, i.e. put values on complexity and quality, and provide a framework for their measurement.

We can group some of the measurements that can be performed on systems into four broad categories:

❏ Product quality

❏ Process quality

❏ How a proposed system will perform

❏ How a system actually performs.

These measurements can either be objective or subjective. In the past, our measurements have been subjective, i.e. Is the user moderately happy with what we have done, and does most of it work? This may be acceptable for a small and fairly trivial system, but for a large and critical system, this subjective measurement will be inadequate, although it is one measurement we may wish to perform. Taking each one of the types of measurement, we wish to establish the criteria against which we are measuring.

Product quality can be a combination of various functions such as ease of use, number of functions left out, extra functions put in at the user's request, number of errors left in, speed of operation etc. We can identify somewhat similar criteria for each of the categories. The only difference is when and where we perform those pertinent measurements, and the use to which we put them in terms of standards and enforcement, as well as the hopeful elimination of projects that exceed expected outcomes in a negative sense. The measurements we take are done at various places in the system life cycle, and should complement those stages we have identified earlier in our adopted SEM.

Associated with design metrics have been various theoretical and empirical methods of analysing our systems.

Code metrics study the final code for complexity, paths, listing and size, in order to determine the quality of the final product. One of the major criticisms of this type of metric is that it is collected too late in the project to be of any influence in the design process. It is, however, useful for assessing the quality of the final product. (See later for an example of code metrics that provide a measure of code quality that we can assess.)

Graph complexity metrics are manipulations of the possible paths that data travels on through a program, module or system. They can, obviously, be collected at the design stage, as we outline either by flow diagram or structure chart, or other means the logic of the program. They can also be put to good use when designing test data to apply to our design, i.e. knowing the possible paths allows us to test for inclusions and exceptions for those paths. The difficulty, however, is that there is a close agreement between the size and complexity of a program, and the possible paths data can take. Hence, we can identify that code size could be a measure of complexity. This is of course not strictly true, as we can all write verbose code when it suits us.

Design metrics, as the name implies, are extracted at the design stage, and are based on the structure of the proposed system. Despite having the best potential for prediction of software quality, little work has been carried out to ascertain its applicability. Therefore, there is little information available on how valid the techniques used are. The techniques themselves are fairly well known, i.e. networks, information flow, coupling and cohesion. We can collect data early on in the design process, and try to correlate this with the results of our efforts when the system goes live. This is done by noting the errors, complaints and alterations, and the time taken to rectify those faults.

Macro metrics are based on completed products, and are often used for resource and cost estimation. There are three main classifications used – parametric, Rayleigh curve based and function based. All are of some value in estimation. There is, however, little validation to support their accuracy, but a considerable amount of empirical data which supports it. Secondly, most of the classifications assume traditional development methods, and will therefore need to be modified to cope with 4GLs, prototyping and dynamic development. Based on the figures for development times, given earlier, we can expect a significant reduction in the time spent to develop a particular application.

Metrics applied earlier in the development cycle can aid us in determining the likely resource requirement, and the quality of the finished product at an early stage. One of the most difficult tasks is to identify those metrics which help us determine, produce and maintain good standards of software quality. Perhaps we can undertake an empirical study of the software projects that we deal with. To do that, those metrics that will be of most interest to us are those concerning design. Bear in mind that these will be specific for the design method that we adopt. They will, however, be of two types; those concerned with the product, and those with the process. The design process will be non-specific, mainly concerned with resource requirements and process change, while the product metrics are centred around the system structure and module design. Most of the data available in the literature relates mainly to systems program and hierarchical decomposition as the method of design. However there is no reason why the design metrics cannot be used for commercial software. Indeed, the example house purchase system given in this book is a full commercial system in use. It has been in use for over a year, and has only just been modified to accommodate new legislation and report requirements. (This should prove to you that no piece of live software is static!)

Measurement of Software Structure

The steps of the methodology we use should identify what measurements to take, and when to take them. By examination of what we do when designing a system, the following measurements can be identified. Measurements relating to the user needs and goals could be attempted. Secondly, quality of software and problems encountered are obvious measures. The time taken to develop functions to undertake meeting initial needs are also valid measures.

System goals all have a set of attributes, an object or function to be undertaken or performed, a purpose, a perspective and an environment in which it will exist. We can redefine these general attributes into a set specific for computer systems. i.e. a statement regarding the assumptions made when designing the function/object. The parameters it expects, gives and works under, constrain the behaviour, measurement and identification of the input/output performed, variables used and the type, accuracy and range which lead in turn to the operational definitions given in the specification for objects, functions, interfaces and variables. See the sample Pascal program later in this chapter.

Measurement of Quality

Therefore, a library of procedures or modules can be kept. Secondly, if the software is such that it is easy to modify then 'pre-written' sections of tested code can be inserted at will in both the prototype and finished product stages.

Table 6.2

Failure Models

Measurement models: The number of failures are measured in operation, and collected together over a period of time. There is no attempt made to rank errors by severity, i.e. there could be a difference in an error that hangs the system, and one that mis-places a title on a report.

Estimation models: Here the software is tested for failures, and is related to historically collected data on failures in other like systems, by comparing the probability of failures against each other.

Prediction models: There is an attempt to make a prediction on the likelihood of failure in operation, based on the characteristics of the software in question, and its operational environment. (These have proved useful when estimating the difficulty of software development.) cf. with complexity measures of algorithms and programs.

There have been several attempts at measures of reliability. Most are based on the methods used in engineering disciplines. These models of reliability have been tried on software. Indeed, certain of the models fit the requirements of hardware suppliers quite well.

The hardware failure rate is normally given in MTBF (Mean Time Between Failures). However, since software does not 'wear out' MTBF should theoretically be infinite. We know from experience that this is not the case, i.e. most software is not perfect, and from time to time lets us down.

By using an adequate SEM we can ensure the reliability of our product. This is by means of an increase in confidence in the end product and, specifically, the reliability of software is designed-in throughout the design and coding process. The end result is tested thoroughly, and specific fault tolerance is specified in fault critical areas. These factors can, of course, be discussed with the end user during the prototyping phase. However, most of these are discussed earlier in the text. The methods used for testing software so far have not. (By testing software exactly we can improve our confidence in it and, hopefully, its reliability.)

Testing is an important and necessary part of the development process, and can take up to 50% of the development effort. This will be true if the application is complex, and the number of tests performed is large. There are various ways of undertaking the testing of software [3]. Unfortunately, when we look at the complexity, different development ideas and techniques it is not possible to produce an ideal or expected solution to a business problem. So, in an SEM, measurement of software quality may not be as exact as we would wish. One way to deal with this is to examine small critical sections of code and measure the quality factors in these, and generally hope that the whole system conforms to them.

Table 6.3

Type of Quality Measure

analysability	testability	comprehensibility	complexity
reliability	modifiability	modularity	economy
simplicity	structure	documentation	layout.

Code Quality

This presupposes that our resulting solution takes the form of generated code. Often we have only generated screens and reports, and the software to form an application from these. However, when we look at code quality, what factors should we bear in mind [6,7]? The following are useful starting points:

❏ The type of variables used, and the specific use to which they are put

❏ The number and type of control structures used, and their use within the program

❏ Transfer of control, and path through the code. (How do we follow that particular path and what conditions are true or false?)

❏ Modularity

❏ Is there a simpler way in which we can write the code?

❏ Comments in the section. Do they:

    a) describe local and global variables; and/or
    b) give a description of the use of statements?

❏ Operand measure (number of statements taken to perform a task) number of variables on RHS vs number of lines.

Remember, a commercial program written in a 3GL may be several hundreds of lines long, so the best we can do is a study a small part of the program or system. Luckily, there are programs that will analyse code and generate the analysis figures for it. Indeed it may be worthwhile writing your own that generates test data lists, if statements, and hence the conditions, path analysis and so on.

Example Pascal Procedures

Two short Pascal procedures will now be listed. Each of these will be analysed in the light of the factors listed above, to identify how we might improve software quality in these specific cases.

Example Pascal Procedure: set_smooth

```
procedure set_smooth(number_of_lines : integer) ;
 { User routine to set the number of line segments per
   curve section
   Argument    number_of_lines The number of line segments
               per curve section
   Global      lines_per_section Storage for the no of
               lines specification blend array size
               max_no_of_lines for blending function values
   Local       u parameter for blending function evaluation
               i variable for stepping through needed curve
               points }
 var
  u : real;
  i : integer;
```

```
begin
  if number_of_lines < 1
    then
      begin
        writeln('Invalid number of lines');
      end;
  lines_per_section := number_of_lines;
  for i := 1 to number_of_lines do
    begin
      { blending function values for middle section }
      u := i/number_of_lines;
      blend[1,i]  := u*(u-1)*(u-2)/ (-6);
      blend[2,i]  := (u+1)*(u-1)*(u-2)/2;
      blend[3,i]  := (u+1)*u*(u-2)/(-2);
      blend[4,i]  := (u+1)*u*(u-1)/6;
    end;
end;
```

Example Pascal Procedure: smooth_poly

```
procedure smooth_poly_abs(x,y,z :store1 ; m :integer);
  { User routine to draw a smooth polygon
    Arguments    x,y,z arrays containing vertices of original
                 polygon
                 m the original number of polygon sides
    Global       blend the array of blending function values
                 bx,by,bz arrays to hold smooth polygon
    Local        nsides number of sides for smoothed polygon
                 j index variable for saving smooth polygon
                 sides
                 k to step through the small segments for
                 each polygon side
                 i,ii variables for stepping through the four
                 sample points
                 l for stepping through the blending
                 functions }
      var
        j,k,i,ii,l : integer;
        nsides : integer;
  begin
    if m < 3
      then
        begin
          writeln('Polygon size error');
        end;
```

```
nsides := lines_per_section * m;
j := 1;
for ii := 1 to m do
  begin
    { Smooth all sides }
    for k := 1 to lines_per_section do
      { smooth a side of the original polygon }
      begin
        bx[j] := 0;
        by[j] := 0;
        bz[j] := 0;
        i := ii;
        for l := 1 to 4 do
          begin
            bx[j] := bx[j] + x[i] * blend[l,k];
            by[j] := by[j] + y[i] * blend[l,k];
            bz[j] := bz[j] + z[i] * blend[l,k];
            if ( i = m)
              then
                i := 1
              else
                i := i + 1;
          end;
        j := j + 1;
      end;
    { Draw the result }
    polygon_abs_3(bx,by,bz,nsides);
  end;
end;
```

Analysis of the two Pascal procedures reveals the following properties:

The set_smooth procedure

Variables:

Types	Name	Purpose
real	u	blending function
integer	i	counter
array	blend	array of function values

Number of control structures: 3
Type of control structures: Begin, end, if, for

Paths through procedure: i) (number_of_lines) < 1
                              :True Error
                              :False do calculations.
                           ii) iteration (number_of_lines)

Simpler algorithm:

To determine if there is a simpler algorithm a careful study of the available literature would have to be done, concentrating on the production of surfaces and curves in CAD systems.

Comments:

These describe local, global variables and give a description of the usage. There are only brief comments in the body of the code. (count the code lines, and comments!)

Operand measure:

Variables: 6 (assume number_of_lines = 1)
No of lines to perform function: 5

The smooth_poly procedure:

Variables

Types	Nature	Purpose
integer	i,ii,l,k,j	steps or counters
	nsides	no of sides
array	x,y,z	data points in space
	bx,by,bz	calculated vertices
functions	poly_abs	draw polygon in absolute space

Number of control structures: 9
Types of control structures: begin end, if then else, for
Paths (m<3)   True : Error
                                    False: proceed with function
(i=m)   True : set i to 1
                                    False: set i to i+1

iterate

For number of sides,
For number of lines per section
For the four vertices.

Simpler algorithm:

Comment as before.

Comments in function:

Describe arguments, local and global variables, and give a description of usage. Again brief comments in body of the function, and numeric counts can be performed.

Operand measure:

Variables:	6 + (no of arrays)
No of arrays:	no of data points * (vertices + blending)
No of lines:	11

Testing Software

As an example, we will write a program that will convert a temperature scale. The conversion is done by selecting a particular conversion routine. We can then try the various methods of software testing that are listed overleaf in Table 6.4.

```
PROGRAM convert
   accept input value for scale 1,2 or 3
   DO CASE
      CASE
         1 PROCESS centigrade
      CASE
         2 PROCESS fahrenheit
      CASE
         3 PROCESS kelvin
      OTHERWISE
   ENDCASE
         display 'Incorrect choice'
ENDPROGRAM convert

PROCESS kelvin
    display 'Input a value in degrees Kelvin'
    accept value
    convert to fahrenheit
    convert to centigrade
    display results
END PROCESS kelvin
```

Table 6.4

Methods of Testing

Functional tests: Testing the individual components of the system from modules to acceptance tests via integration and system function tests.

Path tests: Each path data can take through the system is enumerated, and test data designed to go down that path, including error handling and reporting paths.

Mutation testing: Mutations or small alterations are made in a module which effect the processing of data. The results of these mutations are noted, and compared. (If a mutation causes no serious effects then that module needs further investigation.)

Independent testing: The testing of finished software should be the responsibility of people who have had no part in the task of developing it. Often errors will only come to light at the acceptance stage when the user is actually operating the system.

Philosophy of testing: Debugging is the task that is least tolerated by the programmer. This can cause the software to be full of errors, and not tested in sufficient detail. The assumption should be made that there are errors to be found in any piece of software.

Proof of correctness: The process of proving programs correct causes the manipulation of mathematical symbols, and some tedious clerical work. There has, however, been considerable work done on this aspect of reliability, and program proof [4,5].

The other functions have the same overall structure. The only differences are the conversions made. It may be required that one specifies exactly how the conversions are made in the program, so that the accuracy of the conversion can be determined by potential users. For example, to convert to Centigrade from Kelvin:

```
Centigrade = Kelvin – 273.0
```

The above definition is an approximation to physical definitions of temperature scales. Absolute zero is 0 Kelvin, and the freezing point of water is 0 Centigrade. This should be sufficiently accurate for most users.

Testing Individual Functions/Paths

The program to convert from one temperature scale to another, although simple, displays enough detail to examine the testing techniques as given above. Analysis of the pseudo code or the algorithm should be done to provide an overall structure of the program/module. For our simple program this is given in Figure 6.1

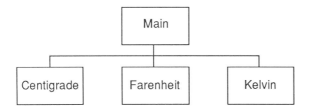

Figure 6.1 Analysis of the pseudo code

The code for the main module can be generated from the design given above. In this case we have used C, but it could be any suitable language. The call of subroutines or functions can be simulated for the purpose of testing with dummy functions or 'stubs'.

Example C program

```
#include <stdio.h>
main(argv,argc)
  int argv;
  char *argc[];
  {
    int choice;
    printf("\n\n\n");/* Send three blank lines */
    printf("Type in 1 for Centigrade conversion \n");
    printf(" 2 for Fahrenheit conversion \n");
    printf(" 3 for Kelvin conversion \n");

    scanf("%d", &choice);/* accept value */
    switch( choice)/* call routine on value */
```

```
     {
       case 1 : centigrade();
           break;
       case 2 : fahrenheit();
           break;
       case 3 : kelvin();
           break;
       default :/* Not correct ? */
         printf("\n\n Incorrect choice ");
       }
}
centigrade()
   {
   }
fahrenheit()
   {
   }
kelvin()
   {
   }
```

Testing the main module:

For each of the possible options 1, 2, or 3 does the program call the respective routines? On any other type of input, numeric (both real integer and negative numbers) does the program display the error message? For any other type of input does the program display the correct behaviour? (ie reject or accept the characters. What about control codes?) After doing the above tests we have tested the main module, and should have an idea as to whether the structure given in the figure is correct, and we have identified four paths in the module:

❏ Selection of the Centigrade function

❏ Selection of the Fahrenheit function

❏ Selection of the Kelvin function

❏ Otherwise display an error.

Each of the functions or subroutines, can be analysed in the same way.

Mutation testing

Consider the function that changes Kelvin input to other temperature scales:

```
kelvin()
  {
  float K,F,C;
  printf("Input a temperature in Degrees Kelvin ");
  scanf("%f",&K);/* accept a temperature */
  if (K < 0)   /* -ve values not allowed */
    printf("\n\nValues <0 not allowed for Kelvin");
  else
    {
    C = K - 273.0;/* Calculate Centigrade */
    F = (K - 273.0) * 5.0/9.0 + 32.0;/* Calculate Fahrenheit *
    printf("\n Kelvin Fahrenheit Centigrade");
    printf("\n%8.2f %8.2f %8.2f", K, F, C);
    }
  }
```

Firstly, construct a set of test data that will fully test the routine. Secondly, make mutations to the routine (the obvious ones are related to the assignment statements!) and apply the same data and note the results, are they as expected? (a suggested set of values is given in the next section.)

Independent Testing

Write a program in any language you wish, test it and correct it to your satisfaction; then give it to a friend to test. I have found that the best testers of software for commercial use are the users, who are often not computer literate. They have, therefore, no preconceptions of what the hardware or software should and should not do. Having set up the software, and generated the test data, monitor the use of the software by the tester. The following list of data should suffice to test the routines in the example C program:

Test	Path	Input values
1	1	0,100,-273,4000,6.78,-10.56
2	2	32,-40,214,5000,89.56,6.789
3	3	0,273,373,80000,100.000,28.67
4	1	-0.0,-400,0.01,48000.99,-273.00
5	2	-0.0,-762.3,0.0,88000.00,3.7567
6	3	-0.0,2.7899,1000000

There is no reason that these values should not be used to test the program with different testing strategies. Also, the values given above only test the program for those values, and we imply from this that it is correct for those values we have not tested for! There is one further point that needs consideration. The program given above is of a scientific nature, and often the results are based on equations, which have as their root physical principles which are only valid over certain ranges, and under given conditions. The full evaluation of the results from such programs is beyond the scope of the book.

Formal Methods

Formal methods in analysis design and programming can be best explained as analogous to the use of mathematics for the development of engineering, i.e. mathematics and engineering can be seen as parallel lines. Formal methods are a way of describing the operation and the result of a programming task in such a way that the descriptions of the data transformations in the statement will provide a symbolic representation in mathematical terms. This can then be analysed and studied in ways similar to the normal mathematical methods of proof and deduction.

Furthermore, as problems become more complex the need for accuracy, reliability and verification grow. There is a move away from the ad hoc testing of software based on a small section of the code towards a more professional and responsible approach to development and testing by the project teams. This is evident in the recent adoption of validation techniques by developers who supply to government departments and the MOD. They require both the produced software and the methods of development to adhere to strict standards, which include formal verification and validation criteria within them. (Certified products!) Enough is now known about the process of design development and production to employ formal methods in projects. Its inclusion in an SEM is a necessity where the client requires it, or as part of the normal process.

From the user requirements we can formally generate a set of specifications using either Z or VDM. However, can this be given to the average user? The difficulty is that despite the efforts of the developers of these formal specifications methods they have not been widely understood (Will the average user or the typical programmer understand the logic and the mathematical constructs used?) Can we, therefore, identify in VDM or Z, or some other formal method, a set criteria that will be helpful to us and the user. In [5] the following is given as a list for the use in implicit specifications:

❏ Direct statement of (multiple) properties which are of interest to the user

❏ Characterising a set of possible results by post-condition (what we expect, and what is true after the process)

❏ Explicit preconditions (what is true prior to execution?)

❏ Less commitment to a specific algorithm

❏ A direct naming of the result.

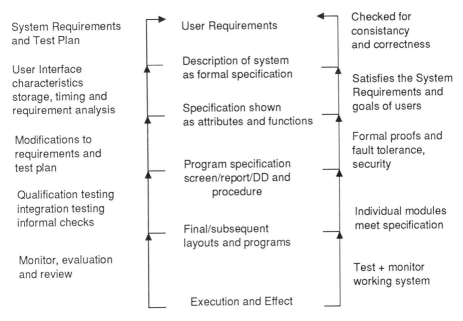

Figure 6.2 SEM and Validation/Verification

Summary

The purpose of formalism is to determine what a system should do rather than how the system performs or works. In this way the specification is implementation independent, and hopefully the software is accurate and reliable, and can be proved to be so. The advent of formalism can be viewed as a two-pronged attack. At one end of the development there are formal methods of specification, and at the other program proofs and verification. However, we can make do without rigorous application of formal methods on most software by using a good SEM, and only using formal methods on critical areas of software, where the algorithm is complex, or there are safety and security issues to be resolved. Again, what we are attempting to do is improve the end users confidence in the product and, hopefully, the system as well.

Exercises

1) Determine the modularity of the Pascal subroutines given earlier in the chapter.

2) There are two rival methods of formal specifications which are in wide use. Reference [10] compares these methods. Can these be used to specify the temperature concersion algorithm (see this chapter) which is given in pseudo code?

References

[1] K. A. Redish and W. F. Smyth, Comparative Descriptions of Software Quality Measures, The Computer Journal, Vol 30, No 3, 1987 pp 228-232.

[2] K. A. Redish and W. F. Smyth, Program Style Analysis : a natural by-product of program compilation, Comm A.C.M. 29 (2), 126-133 (1986).

[3] G. J. Myers, The Art of Software testing, Wiley 1978.

[4] A. L. Furtado T. S. E. Maibaum, An Informal approach to formal (Algebraic) specifications, The Computer Journal 28, (1) 59-67 85.

[5] C. B. Jones, Software Development using VDM, Prentice Hall 1986.

[6] K. A. Reddish and W. A. Smyth, Evaluating Measures of Program Quality, The Computer Journal, Vol 30, No 3, 1987 pp 228 –232.

[7] J. K. Navalakha, A survey of Complexity Metrics, The Computer Journal, Vol 30, No 3, 1987 pp 233-238.

[8] H. K. Berg et al, Formal Methods of Program Verification and Specification, Prentice Hall 1982.

[9] M. S. Deutsch, Software Verification and Validation, Prentice Hall 1982.

[10] D. A. Duce and E. V. C. Fielding, Formal Specification – A comparison of two Techniques, The Computer Journal Vol 30, No 4, 1987.

7

The Data Store

Objectives

Describe the effects of different type of data store.

Identify the effects of the addition of complex data structures, and use.

Description of knowledge bases and database considerations.

Discussion of the fundamental importance of the correct choice of data store.

What is a Data Store?

For the purposes of this discussion the definition of what is a data store needs to be widened to include files, databases, and also knowledge bases. These data stores include not only textual information but also graphical and numeric information in a suitably accessible form. A large number of products are available which allow the design of bespoke systems, and have as their core either a file handler, database or knowledge base. In every system the design of the data store is crucial to the operation and 'look' of the system. In many cases the data store will be a proprietary database system or a file handling system, to which has been added screen and report functions, as well as automatic code generation. They do, however, need to be extended to cover certain requirements that are necessary as part of the inclusion of graphics, and knowledge bases. This is, in practice, difficult to do in the normal transaction processing environment to be found in commercial systems, but is becoming a necessity in modern systems, for example the CAD/CAM database systems that are currently being designed.

One of the most attractive and flexible constructs available for a data store is the 'relational database' [4,5]. Their use has led to the development of sophisticated systems which may be studied as a separate subject [4,5,6]. Until recently, the performance of large, complex databases has been an issue to which suppliers have given a high priority. Most of the problems seem to stem from bottlenecks associated with disk I/O, and database contention. These are areas where careful system design can help solve the problems, or alleviate some of the symptoms.

Table 7.1

Performance Features

Locking and granularity control: This determines the amount of data that is locked for exclusive use, when a particular user requests it. The coarser the granularity the more the database is locked out to other users. Most of the commercially available databases give the designer the ability to lock the database at the table, page and row levels. Therefore when designing a system around such a database it will be necessary to understand the data base management system's (DBMS) locking, and thus allow for minimum contention.

Indexes and keys: The provision of rapid access to the database depends on it's contents. However, contention is increased if the whole of, say, an index is locked out. Therefore, the method of indexing the database is crucial to it's performance. It is, therefore an advantage to have more than one method of ordering the data, e.g. B-tree indexes are good for query and report production, while hash keys are good for update operations. Similarly, the size of the node is important in that the larger the node the more locking is done; the smaller the node the less locking is done (e.g. small B-tree node for intense query processing.)

Variable database page: The number of records in the page is critical, and should be adjusted so as to maximise this number, thus leaving a smaller amount of wasted space, hence reducing I/O overheads.

Buffer size and Number: The number and size of buffers is dependent on the type of transaction that dominates eg small single record transactions may require small buffers, but do not require large numbers of them.

Data clustering: This has a dramatic impact on the reduction of disk I/O. Consider the placement of a customer order on a database system. It is advantageous to keep this and the order lines as close to one another as is possible.

Input and output from the disks on any system is largely influenced and controlled by the database design, and the availability of design options that allow the designer flexibility in data structure representation and placement of data within the structure. Most databases are used by one or more users, each of which create several independent processes contending for machine resources. Therefore, it is implicit in the design of such a system that the data stored in it is carefully designed so as to provide maximum flexibility as well as to minimise the contention. To aid the designer there are built in methods of 'locking' out areas of data, at various levels, 'granularity', and ways of ensuring that the data is placed correctly in the relevant structures [4,5,6,7].

The above issues can be dealt with by fine tuning the resulting data store after its development in the prototype. However, certain issues cannot be left until the later stages of the development process. This is true whether we are dealing with a simple file processing system, or a complex database. Obviously, in the latter case, if our application is running in an existing environment, then we must adjust some of our design requirements to take into account other applications, and their effect on throughput [6]. Similarly, the throughput of a standard piece of software can be critically affected by the file structure we use [7], and the initial design requirements should provide a basis for the formulation of the system's structure, and data.

Characteristics of Files, Databases and Knowledge bases

Figure 7.1 Increase in complexity and structure

The move from one format to the other implies that some amount of structure has been imposed on the raw data, and therefore that structure is fundamental in affecting the processing characteristics of the different data stores. Listed below each main category in Table 7.1 are some of the different structures we can impose on the raw data. The list is by no means exhaustive.

Some of the structures may already be familiar, but some of the implications may not. Also there is usually no one clear structure in all the data that is processed by a particular system. Rather there will probably be several imposed data structures on the raw data during any particular run of the system. It is this fact that has led to the use of more sophisticated methods of storing and representing data during processing.

As an example, computer aided design (CAD) data consists of complex relationships between text, individual graphical items, parts of graphical items and individual drawings themselves. This causes a problem when we wish to store and retrieve information from a CAD database, and several attempts have been made at achieving a fully relational database coupled to a CAD system. Having said this, most bespoke systems will work well alongside the usual DBMS if care has been taken in the analysis and design.

Table 7.1

File Organisations

Sequential: The record is stored in a preset logical sequence, which is based on a set of key fields. This implies that the file is processed in some sort of key order, and records read one after the other.

Direct: The records are again stored in some sort of logical sequence. The individual records can, however, be accessed at will via the same logical sequencing algorithm used for creating that order.

Indexed: The records are stored in a logical order, again based on a set of keys, but the keys and the record-start addresses are stripped from the file, and stored in an index (look up table) which can be accessed in a variety of ways, sequentially, skip sequentially and directly.

Inverted: Most applications order files via a small set of key fields, from which a selection is made for the relevant processing. An important exception to this is when there are no specific key fields, or set of key fields, to be identified. The processing of the file is determined by the user at run time. This means that complex search and selection conditions can be set up by the user for execution. Databases normally have some sort of inverted file structure at their heart, which will cope with this type of access requirement.

Database Processing Characteristics

Since a database is an interrelated set of structures, segments or relationships, the processing characteristics of a particular database are intimately tied to the DBMS and the database architecture. Specific commercial architectures can be studied in the references given, but the general characteristics of using a database need to be given.

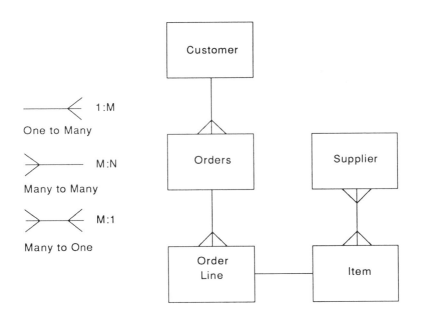

Figure 7.2 Customer orders and items

We have a database which stores customer details, customer orders, items in stock and supplier details. From these simple entities – the **<Customer, Order, Orderline, Supplier, Item>** – we can build a complex set of interrelationships, and hence linkages and structure within any proposed system which we may wish to build. Similarly other data sets relating to entities such as purchase orders, work in progress, and sales can be added to the database at will if so desired. The whole set of information built up becomes the database schema, and this is a description of the organisation's information requirements.

From a description of the whole schema we can construct a small section or sub-schema (see Figure 7.3).

The customer will, hopefully, send one or more orders, which contain requests for us to supply one or more items. Therefore we may wish to write an application to use the data as stored. There are several types of processing that we may wish to carry out on the stored data.

These may seem obvious, but the amount of work that a simple delete operation will trigger is surprising. First we must check that no orders are outstanding, and that any payments due are allocated, then, and only then, can we delete the customer from the database, ensuring in the process that no other application requires this information.

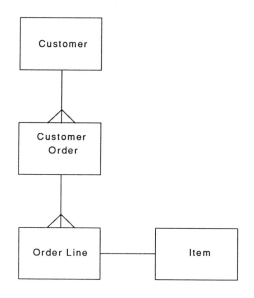

Figure 7.3 Sub-schema for customer orders

Table 7.2

Database Processing

Searching: Looking for an occurrence of one or more entities involves developing a search algorithm that will find these entries based on a field or fields within the entry.

Updating: A database assumes that we can first search for entries, and have valid changes to apply.

Adding: Again the data needs to be correct, and checks made.

Delete: Removal of an entry.

Secondly, the order in which these tasks occur can be handled by the DBMS transparently from the user, and also from programmers if so required. The whole idea is to maintain database integrity. Finally, when the DBMS is satisfied it will schedule the transaction to delete a customer from storage. To sum up:

❏ We wish to delete an old customer from our database

❏ There is an application program that deals with this and also checks to see if this can take place.

❏ The DBMS actually removes the record from storage at some later time.

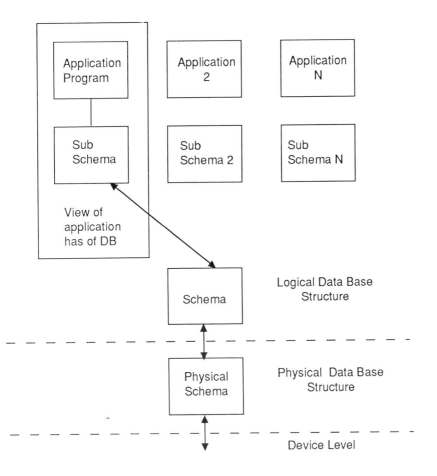

Figure 7.4 Structure of a Data base Management System

In the database there are five ways in which we can think of data representation.

❏ The physical or device level

❏ The storage or storage schema level

❏ The global or logical schema level

❏ The local or sub-schema level

❏ The terminal or end user level.

The analysis of problems that are intended to fit into the overall database concept can be done with an SEM as described, with the additional advantage that most of the lower level operations are taken care of by the DBMS.

Knowledge Base Processing Characteristics

The stages in expert system development can be compared with the normal system life cycle stages found in the 'waterfall' model. These stages were identified in [Hayes-Roth, Waterman and Lenat 1983].

Table 7.3

Knowledge Bases and Expert Systems

Identification: Only some tasks that are performed by the human expert are at present suitable for treatment by expert systems. These must carefully be evaluated in terms of hardware and software requirements.

Knowledge acquisition: The expert's knowledge has to be expressed in some form so as to represent the 'conceptual framework' on which the expertise is expressed. It takes the form of a model which is very dependent on the domain in which the expert system is to be developed.

Design: This involves choosing appropriate data structures, and languages in which to express the model, as well as the interface mechanism between the knowledge base and the expert system.

Development and testing: The implementation and testing of the knowledge base can be a complex task, since the model expressed in the knowledge base is sometimes structured and described in unique ways.

Use: The system is used and modified in use. This needs the provision of continuous modification and testing facilities.

The process of producing an expert system, or a system which uses a knowledge base, is a more complex requirement than the traditional DP system. However, there are similarities in the development process, and therefore the development of the knowledge based expert system (KBES) can benefit from the same SEM as used to produce the usual DP applications. Having stressed the similarities, there are also differences which make the task dissimilar.

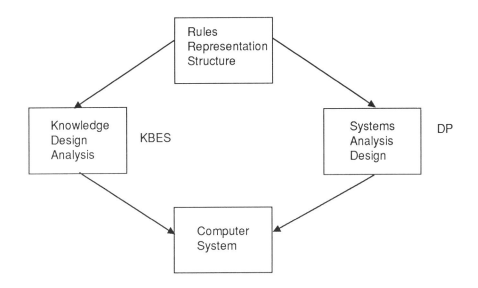

Figure 7.5 Comparison of DP and KBES

The KBES and DP system both use a set of rules representations and structure by which they model the real world. The KBES, however, adds further structure, rules and representations on information, which may already be formatted in the ways common to DP.

As mentioned, the structure of the KBES is intimately tied up to the domain we are trying to model, and the language we are using to describe the model. (The language is not the programming language in which the expert system is written.)

Some common forms of knowledge representation used in expert systems are trees, nets and frames. All of these can be converted to file structures given suitable mechanisms [12].

Record Format and Design

The impact of record format on design should be apparent at its basic level in the initial consideration of the system. Its further impact may not be significant until a working system has been used for some time, and the effect on both processing as well as I/O time will be available. The main need is to try and balance the processing and I/O times of the system, so that system throughput is at an optimum [7]. The timing of processing systems, and subsequent optimisation is beyond this book.

Summary

We saw in this chapter that the development of the application data store is a crucial aspect of the overall design process. One of the criticisms that can be levelled at automatic packages is that they do not allow flexibility when accessing data. However, if these packages can be 'programmed' to allow us to tailor the interface between data and package then this should pose no problem. Secondly the advent of systems where the data is not stored in a recognised file structure, but in a knowledge base, which can consist of various data structures, all of which need designing, has caused problems. The SEM we adopt must be flexible enough to cope with these varying design requirements.

Exercises

1) Draw the data structure of a data set which consists of the names of suppliers, and their short code. The short code to identify the geographical area? Assume that we are only interested in the UK. (Several structures can be used, e.g. a net, a tree, and a relational file structure.

2) Using the book's example of the house conveyancing system, perform a normalisation on the data, and determine the number and structure of the tables. Would this be an acceptable answer for the PC environment?

References

[1] T. Palmer, Software Design and the User Interface, Systems International, March 1987.

[2] E. Edmund, Man Machine Interface, Conference on interdisciplinary information technology, Bradford, April 1988.

[3] Alvey Directorate , Man Machine Interface Strategy August 1984.

[4] C. J. Date, Introduction to Database Systems Vols 1 and 11, Prentice Hall, 1981.

[5] S. M. Deen, Fundamentals of Data base systems, MacMillan, 1977.

[6] M. Vetter, Database Design Methodology, R.N. Maddison, Prentice Hall, 1981.

[7] O. Hanson, Design of Computer Data Files, Pitman 1988.

[8] G. J. Myers, The Art of Software testing, Wiley, 1978.

[9] A. L. Furtado and T. S. E. Maibaum, An Informal approach to formal (Algebraic) specifications, The Computer Journal 28, (1)59-67 85.

[10] C. B. Jones, Systematic Software Development using VDM, Prentice Hall, 1986,.

[11] A. Hart, Knowledge Acquisition for Expert Systems, Kogan Page, 1986.

[12] E. Charniak and D. McDermott, Introduction to Artificial Intelligence, Addison-Wesley, 1985.

8

Management Estimation and Cost

Objectives

Factors relating to project management, and control.

How to analyse costs.

Application of cost models to a practical situation.

Project Management

One of the basic faults in the DP industry is that we assume that a technically capable person is also capable of management. This is not the case! In countries where the distinction is made between management as something one does after spending many years in a technical position, and which needs to be developed and trained for; the productivity of staff, the organisation of people, and the quality of product is better than average. So what can we do to start remedial action? The first thing to realise is that someone who deals with users on a day to day basis, in the form of analysing that user's needs, requirements and wishes, has got some of the required skills for good management. These coupled with additional technical knowledge, subsequent specialised management training, and experience should help.

The additional skills that need to be obtained are centred around people and administration. By administration I mean the ability to control, quantify and allocate tasks, as well as provide resources, advice and backup for subordinates and peers.

There are various ways in which we can assess the impact of our projects on the resources available. The most obvious are cost and time. The usage of resources is affected by the methodology employed, the development environment, the experience of the people concerned, and their morale.

Table 8.1

Project Management Topics

❑ Resource estimation, and the scheduling of those resources, so as to meet deadlines and provide the deliverables.

❑ Organisation and motivation of people to provide a service, and support for users.

❑ Configuration, and management of the hardware and software used to produce the applications and products.

❑ Maintenance management, and quality assurance of new products.

❑ Promotion of standards across products, and the encouragement of production standards such as documentation.

To some extent I have dealt with the quality assurance aspect of software in earlier chapters. There is however, one extra point to bear in mind. Programmers like programming, they dislike testing and documentation. It is therefore necessary to get a strict set of guidelines laid down on how a program or system is to be tested, by whom the system is to be tested and how it is to be tested.

Standards and Documentation

The thing about standards is that there are so many to choose from. Which one do we want? The obvious answer is a set of standards that suit our organisation. There are nationally recognised standards for all sorts of items such as electrical plugs, steel, and paper. There are luckily for us a set of British, American or German standards to which we can write our software, produce our compiler, or test the result. We can abide by these or adopt our own. The user or client may impose a set of standards on us, i.e. the defence industry has its own set of software standards.

The purpose of standards is to enforce a rigorous set of guidelines on the development, production, testing and documentation of a product, and its subsequent monitoring and maintenance. The development standards and production standards have been dealt with by implication. The SEM we choose will have a set of documents which are produced, cross checked, altered, and reissued, thus providing part of the required documentation for the project. The project manager's task is to see that these are delivered on time, and to schedule, and that they are necessary to the functioning of the project. Thus over a period of time a large project will be responsible for the disappearance of a small rainforest. Therefore, we go paperless, and do our development on a computer using a CASE tool or other development environment which allows us to do our thinking on the machine rather than on paper.

The user may want a manual though. Therefore we write one. Part way through a change occurs in the system specification which forces a re-write thus effecting not only the user documentation, but the system documentation as well. The best application systems have on line help, and probably a work through tutorial. The manual itself is produced as a resource for those wishing to use specific commands or options in the system. If the system is at all complex, there will probably be a blow by blow account of the use of the system, with a set of worked examples, and some examples of finished products which are placed in the documentation to assist the user up the sometimes steep initial learning curve. Most micro-based products have got the user manual and the on-line help off to a fine art. It is worth studying these manuals and systems for some ideas on the standards to adopt when writing our own documentation and developing our systems.

Let us take the product dBase III+ from Ashton Tate as an example. The set of manuals consists of two volumes: *Learning and using dBase III+*, and *Programming with dBase III+*. Volume One is intended to lead the user gently through the process of using the product, and contains example uses of commands, functions, and operation of the product. Volume Two is for the more advanced user, and contains more information, and uses of the product as well as example programs. Also, there is a small booklet called *Getting Started dBase III+* for the novice user. Thus, there is a well-structured set of manuals that are intended for the broad spectrum of users that may use the product, from novice to expert.

The documentation for the actual set of programs that go to make up an application is intended for a different purpose. It is intended for the professional developer and maintainer of the developed system. When we design a system, we should bear in mind that the system will have a lifespan, and during that lifespan will need to be maintained by someone. The person that does the maintenance on a commercial system will probably not be the one that actually designed and wrote it. What are the essential components required to perform this task? They are precisely those produced when we design the system:

❏ An overall specification modified as appropriate, so as to incorporate changes to the system over time

❏ A description of the functions, modularity and structure of the product, again modified over time

❏ A description of the data – the structure, type, usage and storage

❏ A picture of the inputs, and outputs produced

❏ A definition and description of the rules which govern the processing

❏ The actual code

Having maintained systems in the past which have been in use for a considerable length of time, the only resort left is the actual program code that is the system, and possibly an overall system description in the form of a flow diagram, or other graphical representation. More often than not documentation is missing or incomplete, and the contents vary in usefulness – another reason for adopting a set of documentation standards.

The advent of more modern development environment, has helped to provide the systems engineer with appropriate tools which can assist in the production of said documentation. (see the chapter containing CASE). Again this idea has come from the micro development environment where there are available productivity tools for the developer. Productivity tools produce documentation of the system based on the sections above. However, to get the full spectrum of coverage for the necessary documentation, one might have to purchase more than one tool to achieve a full documentation set.

Managing Maintenance

The basic cause of maintenance work on software is failure of that software to produce the required responses to the user's requests. These can be identified as follows. The program will not run, it produces incorrect output, the environment in which it operates changes, and finally the addition of extra features it was not designed for. [1]

These type of failures can be categorised and defined closely as 'performance failure', 'implementation failure', and 'processing failure'.

Performance failure is where the system does not meet with the expectations, needs, and requirements of the user. Hopefully by using a good SEM this type of failure will become rare. Implementation failure may be hidden from the user and exists as a set of rules and practices which need to be met in any development. As an example, programming standards may have been dispensed with and the documentation may not be complete. This type of failure is specific to the quality of the final product, not only for the user, but also the implementor. Therefore, we adopt audits of the finished product, and insist that the system is written to internal standards at least, and that the documentation reflects the system in its working state. Finally processing failure, the obvious one. The system terminates, and the termination is caused by 'bugs' in the system. The requirement here is to insist on a proper testing strategy, which will cover at least all the main eventualities and paths through the system.

Having said what causes breakdown, and hinted at the causes, what are the types of maintenance which we should be aware of? These are related to three basic types: Corrective, adaptive, and performance maintenance. ie 'bug fixing', 'adding features', and 'tuning'.

How therefore, do we manage the maintenance. The first idea may be obvious, but surprisingly not many development departments perform such a task. i.e. keeping a maintenance database. We expect programmers to annotate the code when they have made changes. So why don't we extend that idea, and produce a database of that annotation. The information required can consist of a program or system identification, the failure/modification/performance enhancement, the level of the change, who performed the task, when it was done, and the time taken. By keeping such statistics we should be able to identify systems, and programs in systems which cause us maintenance work, and therefore, rectify them as a matter of priority. Secondly we should be able to identify from them the amount of resource we are spending maintaining existing systems.

Whatever the types of maintenance it should at least be done to the same standard as the original system. Your SEM should be able to cope with maintenance of a system. The method may have to be modified so as not to become unwieldy or long winded. i.e. 'maintenance SSADM' is a shorter version of SSADM meant entirely for the maintenance of systems. This assumes that the original system was analysed, designed and documented using the same technique. If it were not then some 'reverse engineering' may be necessary prior to starting the maintenance. Again the course of action is dependent on the size and nature of the modification to the system, and its difficulty and criticality.

Configuration and Management

The usual definition of configuration management is restricted to the control and change management of the system: program, requirements, specifications, and design and analysis documents. In terms of hardware it may be related to how different peripherals are connected to the CPU, and how the CPU resources are managed. I wish to widen the first definition somewhat, and take on board some of the later developments I have mentioned in the book.

There is a need to distinguish when the hardware, software, documentation and requisite clerical or surrounding management system needs to be reconfigured. This may be tied up with the performance criteria of the software, the appearance of the output, the adaptability of the MMI, and changes in environment directly affecting the system and its operation. Of equal importance is the response we give to users. Earlier in the book we saw that the information centre approach to the provision of DP in an organisation was a valid response to the dynamic business world. This can be extended to cover how we organise the development and support teams as well as resource allocation. If users have more say in the development process then they must be considered as part of that team. Secondly the development team will of necessity spend a considerable amount of time working with, and consulting the user of our systems. Thirdly the SEM adopted will cause a varying resource load, the more modern methodologies cause the resource load to come earlier in the project rather than later (performing data analysis, I/O requirements, and entity histories early in the project).

The management of such a dynamic environment can cause problems. One solution is to adopt the team approach to development, i.e. the same team is responsible for the whole of the development cycle. It may even be responsible for requirement specification, and post development support. Secondly expect the team to be away from the office working with the user. We can control this type of project by regular progress meetings, and the adoption of a strategy which governs what is delivered when, and when we meet the project specifications. i.e. All data analysis to be done by a date, Flow diagrams to be discussed changed and agreed by a further date and so on.

Finally give the teams autonomy to make decisions, within the overall strategy of organisational development. Most of the references on this subject treat configuration management as an exercise in controlling software versions. This is only part of the task. Any development goes through a series of versions, each with its set of documentation and software. Each version will probably have a set of dedicated users who may be reluctant to upgrade to later versions of the system they have.

An Example:

Confusion Incorporated has a product that has three versions on release to the software buying public, 2.1, 2.2/a and 3.0. All versions have dedicated users. How can the company keep track of the state of maintenance of each version?

The documentation, programs, maintenance schedules, results and testing have to be kept separately for each version. Therefore, there needs to be a clear set of rules which determine the product, the version, the maintenance and objectives of the task. Each modification we put in will alter the programs, the analysis, the design documents, and the user manuals to a greater or lesser extent.

The solution is to enforce discipline on the development team, so that minor alterations are reported and acted on at the same time and in the same release or patch as the larger ones. The larger maintenance items must go through the same acceptance criteria as a new or proposed system, and be assessed as to the likely impact on the system. Remember also that while the project team is bringing out a new version of a product, the business needs of the users will be changing. All projects go through a series of stages no matter what SEM we use. These are the identifiable checkpoints or deliverable items in the development. Therefore these changes will effect these items – the later the change in the project's life the greater the cascade effect in the deliverables at the system checkpoints. The stages in development, checkpoints or deliverables are identifiable in our chosen SEM:

❑ The system specification in terms of the user requirements as agreed by the prospective user of the system

❑ The plan of production for the system giving the cost benefit analysis, and well as projected resource requirements

❑ The complete software requirements specification in terms of a model either on paper or executable prototype

❑ The outline user manual or online help system

❑ The system design both preliminary and final

❑ The resulting programs duly annotated, and the executable programs

❑ The test schedules data and results

❑ Operation and installation manuals and procedures

❑ The final user manual(s) and/or on-line help system

❑ The system maintenance documents consisting of known problems, work arounds, requests for action, and orders for change.

In a large development it may be a full time task to keep the versions of an existing system documented, and the subsequent program versions accurate. This is why it was addressed as a requirement for a CASE tool. Secondly not only does the above list concern the documentation, but it should also incorporate the work that goes into producing each stage, so that everyone connected with the product knows at which stage the product is at, on which version they are working, and what is expected of them.

Organisation of People

The task of a project leader, chief programmer, or DPM is essentially a task of management. [2] There are three basic types of managers: those which manage production, those which cope with the changes in the business environment, and those which lie somewhere in between, and keep the warring factions apart. These are technical, institutional, and organisational respectively. Compare this with the original definition of systems given earlier and you will see that the systems view of the organisation ties up quite well with the view of management given here. Therefore, the system engineer must be able not only to recognise the type of system, but also the management style it is likely to fit into.

Secondly the type and structure of the team put together to develop a system may have a direct bearing on the finished product. Remember however, that people are motivated in their employment by more that pay and conditions. They need recognition and a sense of belonging to a group. Since attitudes to work are strongly influenced by the group then the selection, motivation, and work pattern of the group is important. It takes on further significance in systems work, since the group or team is the usual development strategy. *(Reference [7] contains an introduction to management issues for business, and is a suitable introduction to the management of an organisation and how management operates in the business environment.)*

The following is a suggested ideal structure for a development effort of medium to long term. For shorter, less costly development it would be too cumbersome.

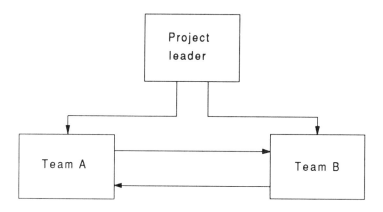

Arrows indicate interchange of members
from Team A to B and back

Figure 8.1 The ideal development team

The sample structure should not be seen as fixed, it is meant to illustrate an ideal. The structure should be viewed as a fluid entity, the membership of which can vary according to the needs of the project. Taking on more members when required, shedding members, and adjusting the make up of the project team by co opting members with specific skills.

The team leaders take on a critical role in this type of structure, responsible for the managerial aspects of the project development, but also to be considered as one of the team, producing the requisite technical output when appropriate. Secondly they should be available and in control at all critical stages of development, particularly at the quality review stage. Under the project leader are four to six other team members, split into groups of two. However, they can be dynamically allocated tasks which require fewer or more people to perform. e.g. pairs for diagramming or singularly for normalisation and data analysis. On a large project the development may be done by many such teams, all interacting and producing sections of the system.

After analysis and design, the next stage is to code the system using the appropriate design documents to the required coding specification, as laid down in the organisation's standards. For this purpose the structure of the team is similar to the above, with the project leader becoming a chief programmer, and the subordinates working on different program modules. There have been other structures suggested for this stage of the development, and the roles of team members have been identified [8]. I have paraphrased the functions expected of the team members, so that they are related to task specifications rather than people, as follows:

❏ The chief programmer who defines the specifications for the programs to be written. i.e. functions, performance, design, testing and documentation. The assumption is that he or she will work with the most up to date programming environment possible, and can be an active member of the team if so required.

❏ The administrative secretary who removes administrative burdens from the chief programmer, and may even performs this task for more than one project team.

❏ The documentation editor, who checks final draughts of all documentation prior to release.

❏ The team clerk who undertakes the task of submitting programs to the machine in the correct order, channelling all output back to the relevant team members, coordinating the documentation, and ensuring that all team members are on the relevant release or version of software, and documentation.

❏ The bit juggler who delights in the nitty gritty of development, and delves into the depths of the target machines operating system, compilers and peripheral drivers, writing specialist sections of code for the team, and possibly other teams. The juggler should also write tools for use in projects, which can be collected together to form general use libraries that can be included in many projects.

❏ The program buster who tests pre-release versions of software to destruction, writes the test routines, designs the test data and acts as 'devil's advocate'.

❏ The language expert who can remember the most obscure syntax in the chosen development language, and acts as a consultant to the rest of the team.

One obvious criticism is that if each of the functions above represented a person's job, then it would be too large. The large team approach may be counter productive, in that the more people thrown at a project the more the project slips, due to the communication problem between staff, and the shear inertia of such a group. On a large project a lot of time is spent on consultation, and formal review meetings, to ensure that all project team members know exactly what they are supposed to do and when.

Secondly it may be that the design team and the end user are also included in the consultation process, thus causing further communication problems. The project may still have the problems as discussed in chapter one. We need a flexible approach to the development of large software projects. The team developing the system needs to take on board the analysts, the designers, users and implementors of the system. Hence the adoption of a de-centralised development method in most organisations. Secondly the team chosen should as far as possible be responsible for the development from feasibility to implementation and handover to the user department.

Lastly the functions identified above can be carried out by a smaller group of people, the team members taking on many of the functions, and even the end user performing several of the administrative tasks regarding analysis and design documents. Again the ideal size of a programming team seems to be around six members[8]. This optimum size can increase or decrease as the project progresses, or as special requirements force a change in the resource loading.

Resource Estimation and Scheduling

How to analyse costs

The analysis of costs attached to any systems development, is perhaps one of the hardest tasks which can befall us, not because it is difficult, but because the ground rules are forever shifting. There have been numerous attempts in the past to identify factors which will allow us to estimate the likely cost of development, based on a set of models which we employ, a dose of judgement, and a lot of experience. What is wanted is a cost of production, and an analysis of the possible benefits which will accrue with the completion of the project. To perform this task we may have to study alternative strategies and solutions. We may also have to present our findings in such away as to quantify the benefits, even if those benefits are not immediately definable in terms of hard cash.

Checking the alternative designs and options

Production of design alternatives presupposes that we have the time to produce these alternatives, and that the customer's requirements are loose enough to allow some leeway in our solutions. First of all, we must undertake an analysis of the alternatives based on their impact on the personnel involved, the available resources at our disposal; the required and projected computer time for development. We must also monitor the organisational performance both prior to adoption of the system, and its likely alteration and change post-adoption; finally the overall organisational goals should be assessed, based on the company's business strategy and requirements.

After performing the initial analysis several alternatives will probably be abandoned, or rejected as not being feasible technically, economically or politically. The remaining alternatives can then be costed tentatively, so as to provide us with costs of operation, organisational impact, as well as development and implementation.

Costing Methods

To provide these cost and resource estimates we can use a variety of models, we will limit ourselves to three such models, but there are others. Firstly the software productivity data approach, this method of estimating costs is based on historical data, and experience of the estimator, but is also governed by the following factors, which effect software productivity, and hence the cost of software produced.

Table 8.2

Factors effecting software productivity

❏ The size and expertise of the development organisation.

❏ The complexity of the problem to be solved.

❏ The number and type of changes in the requirements, design, and constraints that are applied to the project.

❏ The analysis and design techniques used.

❏ The technical resources available, languages, compilers, hardware, development tools, and environment.

❏ The reliability and performance of the trial computer for computer based systems.

❏ The review and quality assurance measures offered and used.

These various and diverse factors could lead us to the conclusion that software guesstimation is a 'black art' rivalling necromancy, palmistry, and crystal ball gazing. There is however the possibility that we can use data for other projects that have been completed, and are of a similar nature. We can also employ some further costing techniques which help us to produce a model on which we can base the cost estimation:

❏ Delay definite costing until late on in the project, and only use historical data to obtain the go ahead.

❏ Develop a parametric model of the software cost, again based on existing software, costs and expectations.

❏ Use decomposition techniques to generate costs in dissimilar ways.

❏ Use an automated costing system, which we can tune.

If we delay the costing of the project to near its completion, we are certain to be more accurate than if we attempted to do it earlier. The penalty for this is that we have no target at which to aim, and we may run into extra development costs and time.

Furthermore the resource requirements need careful consideration prior to the beginning of a project. If we didn't perform an estimation as to the resource requirements we may run the risk of allocating too few, or too many staff to each project. If we had an infinite amount of time, and other resources, then this approach would be all right, but as we are in the real world we haven't, and hence this approach to resource and software cost estimation is not recommended.

The parametric model based on collected historical data, and the life cycle of many projects is an average indication of the resource loading of projects. However, we may have some difficulty in determining the magnitude and type of the parameters we need to consider to model our prospective system cost. As an example consider the Putnam Norden model [9] for resource deployment. This is based on the Rayleigh curve, which has been found to be a good fit to actual data.

The unfortunate thing is that in a system development the resources are not applied smoothly throughout a project, but are applied in a stepwise fashion. Secondly this type of estimation is tied quite closely to the more traditional approach to systems development, and gives expected project milestones in terms of the serial or waterfall methodology [9].

We can make this more accurate by splitting or de-composing a large project into smaller more manageable parts, thus making them more understandable. thus allowing us to make accurate predictions on the resource loading required to fulfil the large project.

To estimate the resource usage of a proposed project, we need to know quite a lot about the project, and make the assumption, sometimes false, that it is possible to achieve computerisation. (The failures can be spectacular!). Also, the best technique for one particular system may not be appropriate for all systems, and for all development teams.

One way of counteracting this is to perform the resource estimation using several techniques, find the average, and a variance from the average, and quote that as the expected resource loading. Again we can split the larger projects up into smaller sections. The split is a matter of choice, but it is probably best done by functional area and development methodology deliverables. Thus, the sectionalising of the project can be done on a modular basis, increasing the accuracy of our predictions[10,11,12,13].

One of the difficulties with these types of model is that they require tuning for a particular development environment, and also need a fairly large historical database on which to assess the accuracy of the tuning parameters. A topical area is that of combining a heavily mathematical model such as COCOMO or SLIM with an encapsulated expert system. There are packages now available that will perform this on a desktop micro.

Estimation and Costing Models

There are many possible models, and here we present a small selection of the more popular, in the briefest possible manner.

The **resource model** [3] uses data collected from a variety of projects over a period of time. The simplest version is the static single variable model:

A resource is designated with a constant K. Applied
to that resource is an estimated characteristic. Therefore
an expenditure of that resource is give by:

Resource = K * (Estimated characteristic)

From this a variety of resources can be estimated [3]:

E	=	$5.2 * L^{0.91}$	Effort in person months (E)
D	=	$4.1 * L^{0.36}$	Duration in calendar months (D)
D	=	$2.47 * E^{0.35}$	Staff size on project (S)
S	=	$0.54 * E^{0.6}$	Lines of documentation (DOC)
DOC	=	$49 * L^{1.01}$	Number of lines of source code (L)

Figure 8.2 Static Single Variable Model

A refinement is the *multivariate* model. This makes use of the database of collected values for the resources required, then fits the polynomial to those values.

Resource = $K_1 * e_1^{C1} + K_2 * e_2^{C2} \ldots K_n * e_n^{Cn}$

Figure 8.3 Static Multivariate Model

The Rayleigh-Norden curve is used to generate a 'Software Equation', denoted by L (delivered lines of code) in Figure 8.4:

$L = C_kK^{1/3}td^{3/4}$, where:

L = Delivered lines of code

C_k = State of the art technology constant and is a reflection of programmer throughput:

   6,500 – poor software development environment (batch)
   10,000 – good environment (on line)
   12,500 – excellent environment (automated tools)

K = $\dfrac{L^3}{C_k^3 t_d^4}$

t_d = development time in years
K = development effort in work units

Figure 8.4 Dynamic Multivariate Model[4]

The **N.C.C. time estimation Model** estimates the man-months as the sum of:

   2.57 * Number of Output Formats

   5.1 * Number of Record Types

   0.12 * Number of Input Formats

Functional points estimation[6] uses the following parameters to estimate man-months:

   I = Number of External Input types

   O = Number of External Outputs

   E = Number of Enquiries

   P = Number of External Files (Program Interfaces)

   F = Number of Internal Files (Those Generated, and used by the program)

$F_p = 4*I + 5*O + 4*E + 7*P + 10*F$

The effects of adopting a 4GL on software productivity have been quantified for the various project aspects and are reported [5] to be:

	4GL	**COBOL**
Analysis	1.0	1.0
Design	4.0	1.0
Documentation	6.0	1.0
Programming	7.0	1.0
Testing	20.0	1.0
Implementation	1.6	1.0

The total productivity gain over traditional programming languages can be significant – in the above, the averge gain is 5.3 compared to COBOL. This figure is low compared to the survey carried out in July 1985 by Price Waterhouse, where an overall productivity gain of 6.5 is quoted. The interesting productivity gain in testing, is one that may not have been expected, since 4GLs are sold on their ability to increase programmer productivity. They do increase the productivity significantly, but not to the extent we may be led to believe. The initial stages of development are also disappointing. It is in this area where CASE tools are hopefully going to make an impact on the development process.

As an example, let us consider the system that we have continually used throughout the book, and estimate the likely cost based on two models:

NCC model: 2.57*8 + 5.1*3 + 0.12*2

i.e. 8 output formats (6 reports 2 screens)
    3 record types (1 masterfile 2 ancillary files)
    2 input types (1 master input, 1 ancillary input)

= 36.1 man months

Functional point model:

$I=2$ $O=8$ $E=3$ $P=2$ $F=3$

$F_p=$ 104 man months

The actual project took two man months from start to finish (implementation). It was written in a 4GL on a micro computer, and the specifications changed twice during development. So what is wrong with the estimating models? The reason is this the above estimation models are based on the 3GL and waterfall SEM and development method. They also assume a poor environment. The 4GL used to develop the system could also be used to prototype the system for the user, and illustrate its possible functions.

Secondly, skeleton procedures existed for the system in general. The only programming as such was the fitting together of the procedures in a logical manner, the painting of screens and reports, and the disposal of remaining bugs.

A better fit for the development system used is as follows:

> 6 * No of screen/reports or definitions.
> 2 * No of record types in database or files.

+ 10% to 25% contingency, which is dependent on the number of menus and expected project difficulty. e.g. if external calls to routines that use traditional languages are needed then use the higher value.

Using the above figures for the house purchase system we obtain the following results:

> 6*10 + 2*3 = 66 hours + 15% contingency = 75.9 hours.

This is a better approximation to the actual figure for development. If a quote is intended then do not forget to add on to this figure overheads, profit and VAT. Remember also this method of assessing is applicable to my development environment, and this essentially simple system.

Summary

In this chapter I have tried to introduce two themes – project management and resource estimation. Often the two go hand in hand, and the project manager is responsible for the estimation, allocation and control of resources throughout the project. Hence it is an obvious addition to any book on systems engineering. The topic of management itself is complex, and it is best left to the reader to undertake further study in this direction.

The subject of software cost is, as we have seen, very complex, and it is by no means a straightforward matter to assess the expenditure of resources in any one particular project. Yet again the hope is that by careful consideration and some experience we can increase the effectiveness of our estimation methods. The result is that the software engineer needs experience, and the only way to obtain experience is to do.

Exercises

1) Use any feasibility study or outline of a project with which you are familiar, and perform the resource estimations on it. Then compare these with the finished item.

2) Why should the optimum number of people in a team be similar to the optimum number of procedures in a program?

3) Try to identify the function points in any software project, allocate the staff to those function points, then compare this with the Rayleigh Norden curve.

References

[1] E. Burton Swanson, The Dimensions of Maintenance, I.E.E.E. Proc. of 2nd International Conference On Software Engineering, 1976, pp 492-497.

[2] Thomas A. Petit, The Behavioural Theory of Management, Academy of Management Journal, 1967, pp 341-350.

[3] A Method of Programming Measurement and Estimation, IBM Systems Journal Vol. 16 No 1, 1977, pp 54-73.

[4] A general Empirical Solution to the Macro Software Sizing and Estimating Project, I.E.E.E. Trans on Software Engineering Vol. 4, No4 1978, pp 345-361.

[5] Nick Gill (Pro-Lab), 4GL Productivity gains, Systems International, June 1987.

[6] Albrecht and Gaffney, Functional Points for software cost estimation, I.E.E.E. Trans on Software Engineering, Vol. 9, No 6,19, pp 639-648.

[7] Roger Oldcorn, Management: A fresh approach, Pan, 1982.

[8] F. P. Brooks, The Mythical Man Month, Addison-Wesley, 1975.

[9] L. H. Putnam and A. Fitzsimmons, Estimating Software Costs, Datamation, Sept 1979, pp 189-198, Oct 79, pp 171-140, Nov 79, pp 137-140.

[10] B. W Boehm, Software Engineering Economics, Prentice Hall, 1981.

[11] B. A. Kitchenham and N. R. Taylor, Software Development Cost Estimation, The Journal of Systems Software, Vol 5, 1985 pp 267-278.

[12] A Comparison of Cost Estimation Tools, Proc of 8th International Conference on Software Engineering, pp 174-180.

[13] A. M. E. Cuelenaere et al, Calibrating a Software Cost Estimation Model: Why and How, Vol 12, 1987, pp 558-567.

9

CASE STUDY: Scenario and Tutor's Guide

Barchester County Council Community Charge and Rent System

Framework

The discussion here is based on the work of Romisowski 1981. Four types of knowledge can be identified:

FACTS	Knowing objects, events or people
PROCEDURES	Knowing what to do in a given situation
CONCEPTS	Being able to give instances to define concepts

Four types or domains of 'skill' can be identified:

COGNITIVE	Intellectual skills in applying knowledge
AFFECTIVE	Attitudes and value systems
INTERACTIVE	Behaviour in group situations
PSYCHOMOTOR	Physical skills needed

Using these ideas he goes on to propose a skill continuum as follows:

Table 9.1

Skill Domain	Reproductive Skill Application of Procedures	Productive Skill Application of Principles
COGNITIVE	Applying a known procedure to a known problem	Solving a new problem by developing a new procedure
AFFECTIVE	Conditional emotions and attitudes	Self control in furtherance of goal
INTERACTIVE	Conditional social habits leadership	Interpersonal control supervision
PSYCHOMOTOR	Repetitive or automatic physical action	Planning appropriate physical action

Table 9.2

Ideal set of skills of computing staff

❑ Identify problems or needs which are not immediately apparent

❑ Help others to clarify their problems or needs

❑ See dynamic interrelationships between areas of technical knowledge

❑ Understand the aims of specialists, know when to call on their skills

❑ Formulate and undertake a search in many areas of knowledge

❑ Produce a body of relevant knowledge concerning the problem at hand

❑ Organise manage and monitor a project

❑ Define courses of action and make a rational choice from these

❑ Maintain records of thoughts and actions

❑ Communicate ideas and instructions to others

❑ Be self critical about tasks done and decisions made

❑ Interact profitably with others in furtherance of common ends

❑ Share work loads and responsibility within a group

Case studies can be used in a variety of ways in formulation of computing and Information system skills, and particularly Systems engineering training. One of its main uses is in the simulation of a real problem, to allow the students the facility of learning in a structured environment. The learning can be controlled and the outcome studied and discussed against a controlled or suggested outcome. The main need of students, trainees and practitioners in systems engineering is one of experience in development of a system. This is also true of computer staff in general, and by using the ideas presented in Table 9.1 opposite we can identify those skills required by computer staff, most of which will be of particular significance to the Systems Engineer (see Table 9.2 opposite).

Obviously other methods can be used to produce the designed or desired skill level. However the case method is very good at quickly producing people with a *principle* knowledge and good level of productive skill quickly. It also provides a vehicle by which to substantially increase experience without exposing the trainee to the risk of a *live* project.

Aims of Case Study

❑ To develop problem solving and decision making skills

❑ To give insight into complexity of 'real world' problems

❑ To foster development of personal conceptual framework

❑ To sharpen analytical judgement skills

❑ To develop skills in self organisation

❑ To develop interactive skills

❑ To expose people to risk under controlled circumstances.

Coupled with the above aims one should generally look at the types of case study available to help achieve those stated aims, and more specifically fits in with the SEM used.

There are four categorisations of case studies which are applicable to Systems work:

Area of work   The type of skill one wishes to produce, a level of understanding, state of work level of work, level of integration into SEM and other organisational practices.

Method of use   Real/made up, treatment of study ie discussion, appraisal, illustrative. The of individual participants involvement, simulation, role play, incident or incomplete solutions or examples.

Reasons for use	Introduction to a course, part of overall training in an organisation. Dissemination of skills ideas and method.
Types of Case study	Case exercise: a small structured specific area of study. Case history: a detailed account of an implementation. Case project: a large, open-ended analysis and design.

Considerations of Make Up and Management

The case study as such can be used at any stage to illustrate the points of a particular SEM. It can also be used as an example of the types of problems and projects which are to be met within practice. This can include notes and suggested outline solutions to the problem. However the basic material examples of original documents may or may not be given, but can be produced to suit the SEM.

Similarly the actual detailed solution, and specific methods may not be prescribed in detail, only outline methods, and solutions can be presented as a guide. Thus any case study can be presented as a course project, or as a series of exercises throughout. The solution outlined in this chapter is presented to illustrate some of the tools described earlier. Thus they act as a guide to the analysis, design and implementation of a system.

The stages within the case study should be used in conjunction with specific chapters in the rest of the book. The exception to this is the feasibility report. This is presented in its entirety as a point for discussion and to lay the ground rules for further development. The feasibility study presented is the actual document produced by the DP department of a large city council, and illustrates quite nicely the structure and detail required in such documents.

Contents of Case Study

Scenario	Scene setting and background information.
Guide	Specific information regarding roles, volumes documents and structure of study.
Proposed Solution	Outline possible solution.

Management of Case Study

This section is included to suggest the necessary logistics, and assessment of any answers, set against the following factors:

| Logistics | Administrative duties, timetabling, project rooms effort, assimilation and maintenance of material, and experience of participants. Rate of progress; suggested outline solutions. |
| Assessment | Assess elements of the study (pass/fail) setting milestones or deliverables (dependent on methodology). Written final profile. Assessment critique of participants, peer group discussion and review. |

The method of assessment used is a matter of choice, but one of the best methods is to assess the milestones in the method used to analyse the example. If, for instance, the participants decide to use SSADM to solve the problem, the expected milestones are specified by that method. Bearing in mind that the feasibility study has been done, the project can be used for stage 2 and 3 of SSADM namely Systems Analysis and Systems Design. Even if a more flexible project is envisaged then there must be a set of checkpoints so that there can be an assessment of progress, and a comparison with expectations as outlined in the feasibility study.

Scenario

Case Study: Barchester City Council Rent and Community Charge

Barchester City Council (BCC) computing committee

Background

The council is a fairly large urban/semi-rural council that collects rents and charges from householders, tenants, and business people. Some 500,000 people live within the BCC boundary, and about one third pay rents of some sort, while a further quarter pay water charges, and other service charges directly to the council. Most people pay the community charge CC. (No consideration is given here to the collection of the Business Charge.)

The council's policy towards its tenants is enlightened, and it attempts to look after both rent and CC payers to the best of its ability. Traditionally the city has been split into five districts, and the rural part into three large areas. Some of the urban districts have a number of small rural areas included. Therefore, the five districts include several small villages around the periphery of the city. The eight areas along with the central office form the administrative areas that go to make up the city.

The computing committee was set up last year to centralise and steer the council's IT policies. One of its objectives was the modernisation of the administrative function, by adoption of modern technology where possible. One of the first areas identified was the rent and CC accounting system which was in urgent need of modernisation – the old system based on manual receipting and batch processing.

The organisation of the Rents/CC office is shown in Figure 9.1, the chief housing officer being directly responsible to the elected authority, i.e. the Housing committee of the council. The chart shows the main structure of the council's rent and CC accounting function. There are of course other staff involved in such a large undertaking.

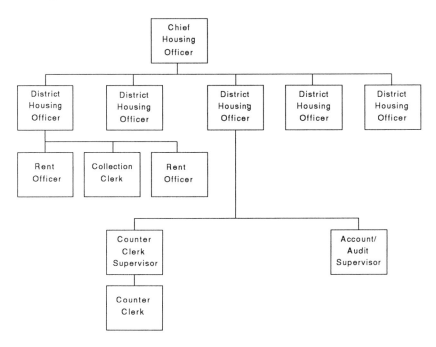

Figure 9.1 BCC Rent and CC office structure

The members of the council staff work a five day week, working hours are 0800 to 1800 hours on a flexi time basis at the central district, and the offices are open to the public from 0930 to 1200 and 1300 to 1600 hours.

Rent and Community Charge

On 17th July the computer sub committee initiated a feasibility study into the new computerisation of Housing rents under the broad headings of:

❏ Collection

❏ Arrears collection

❏ Rent and Community Charge.

The system was to cater for 150,000 properties with a growth rate of around 10%, and the agreed cost was to be in the region of £100,000 development cost and £250,000 per annum running cost excluding the machine(s) maintenance costs.

Collection of Rent and Community Charge

The authority wishes to maintain the good relationship it has with tenants, by being as flexible as possible with regard to payment method and times. At the present time the city areas are split into estate office districts from which collectors go and collect rent and charges from the tenants. Tenants can also go to these district offices and the central office and pay directly. These payments can be made on a weekly or monthly basis. The other possible methods of collection are by direct debit, directly from salary for council workers, bankers draft, and of course personal cheque. The amounts collected at the district office are sent to the central office for processing, and the records updated accordingly. The CC is normally assessed once per year, and collected bi-annually from each payer. Other methods of payment are also accepted but whatever the method the payments can only be made to the central office.

If any tenant of the CC payer falls behind with payments the office issues a warning note. However, if there is an unforeseen circumstance causing difficulty in the payer's record, this is taken into consideration. Arrangements can be made by the housing officials for reductions in, and re-scheduling of, payments. A note is made of the re assessed payment, and a new calculated amount due is issued to the payers.

Arrears collection

Other than those cases mentioned above, all tenants can make up any shortfall over an agreed length of time. Where a series of payments is missed, and the ability to pay has been shown, after a first warning letter as above, a subsequent letter in red is sent. If no payment or explanation is forthcoming within 10 working days, this is followed by a severe warning letter. If again this is ignored after 20 working days, a solicitor's letter is sent, and proceedings initiated to recover the missing amount.

Rebates

These can be arranged by tenants or charge payers with a simple interview with housing staff, and a form and supporting letter from the DHSS. The council will try to accommodate reduced and non payment of amounts due by citizens, and will only take legal action in the most severe cases.

Responsibilities of Key Staff

Chief Housing Officer   **Nigel Williams**

Responsible for: Collection of rents and charges
Issue of writs and collection of debts
Authorisation for major construction and repairs
Reporting and Audit of the rent and charge collection.

District housing Officers	**Silvia De Fratas, Jim Croft,Thomas Grangewell, Simon Kirk, Megan. Cliff, Trudy Jones, Sandra Smiley, and Gloria Tagget**

Responsible for:
Rent collection in estate offices
Supervision of rent collection
Issue of the first warning letter
Accounting for district estate rents.

Deputy Housing Officer   **Charles Beacroft**

Responsible for:
Rent and CC collection at the central housing office
Reporting of bad debts
Audit of estate offices collection
Supervision of all counter clerks
Sending out of overdue payment after 10 working days.

Office Counter Clerks

Responsible for:
Collection of money paid by tenants and CC payers
Issue of receipts and updating of records
Issue of receipts to payments made by post and other methods
Sending out the first letter of warning.

Audit Supervisor   **Malcom Tickall**

Responsible for:
Production and auditing of district and central yearly accounts, and the systems that produce those accounts.

Guide to the Case Study

Method of Use

The case study concerns the collection of rents and charges by BCC. The present ad-hoc system of rent collection and accounting is based on historical boundaries, and a largely manual system, with some computerisation at a central site. The collection methods are partly based on automatic bank debits, cash collection direct from tenants, and direct payments of other kinds. The variations in collection methods in the different districts have caused problems in the past, and have lead to inaccurate accounts. Hopefully any new system will rationalise collection methods, update the current computer system, and bring rigour into the accounting and audit of rents as well as the community charge levied.

Tenant: Mrs J Archer

Address: 21 Brookfield Close
Barchester BA2 1JT

Reference:

District:

Weekly amount:

Date	Amount	Initial	Date	Amount	Initial	Date	Amount	Initial	Date	Amount	Initial

If found, return this card to the Barchester Council Offices

Figure 9.2 An example of a rent card. The reverse has the address of the tenant and the postal address of the Council offices

Barchester Council has set
the general Community Charge
for the year ending 31st March 1990

Date of demand: 1 Apr 90
Telephone: 055 7343
Reference: BAZ1JT38 363 008

Payable in accordance
with instructions
overleaf

Mr J Archer
21 Brookfield Close
Barchester BA2 1JT

Period of demand
1 Apr 1990 to 31 Mar 1991

House and Land

Authority	Barchester Council	Water fees	Police	Fire	Total due
Amount	260.00	57.36	38.29	28.63	**384.28**

Payment 1: Due date 30th Apr 1990

Amount due: £192.14

Received   Date:

Paymen 2: Due date 30th Oct 1990

Amount due: £192.14

Received   Date:

Figure 9.3 Community Charge bill

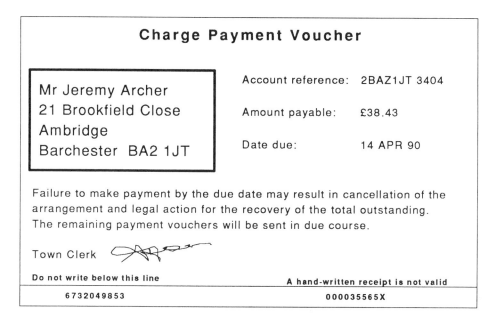

Figure 9.4 The Community Charge payment receipt

The difference between the collection of rents and community charge will also be a problem. Up to now the rating system has been centralised, and rate payments have had to be made to the civic hall either in person or by post. This needs to be looked at in the light of the decentralisation of the renting system, and the variety of methods of more automatic payments.

Payments made to the civic hall from no matter what the source are always liable to the usual portion of bad debts, and while genuine cases of hardship in payments are accepted, it is envisaged that stricter controls of indebtedness are to be introduced. Secondly, advice regarding rent and charge arrears is to be available via the usual offices

BCC wishes to automate and decentralise the collection of rent and community charge payments, as well as modernisie the existing computer system. For this reason it has recently appointed a team of Systems Engineers to produce a design for the new computerised accounting system, and also to advise on the management and clerical procedures to be performed on a decentralised collection system. It is the task of the group to analyse the documents presented, and propose a solution to the BCC computing committee.

The scenario and the documentation that follows provide enough information for a project to be completed. The implementation of the project may be done using a variety of methods, such as interviews with staff undertaking roles of the main protagonists, production of the correct current documents used in the system, and primarily the feasibility study. The participants in the case study may be split into groups of four or five based on the model given.

Size and Composition of the Groups

When building groups, take into consideration the following constraints:

❑ Length of experience of the participants in a variety of fields not necessarily IT

❑ The applications and machines worked on if any

❑ The age and maturity of the participants

❑ The ability to communicate to others

❑ Leadership skills of the participants.

Suggested Timetable

The exact timing would be dependent on the makeup of the group, and the length of the course. The following times are a suggested minimum assuming the group size set at four individuals:

Introduction of the Case Study by the course leader	1 hr
Group work on the material presented in the Scenario, feasibility study, and Appendix III	3 hrs
Review of work in groups	1 hr
Preparation for design and analysis	2 hrs
Analysis and design of new system	26 hrs
Presentation of findings by group	0.5 hr
Discussion of solutions	5 hrs

Tutor/Presenter

One person should act as a guide to the participants throughout. It is essential that the detail is presented to the participants in such a way that it is related to the experience, and the local attitude of the groups. The tutor or presenter while having the required skills to design the system, should try not to impose any views on the participants.

Objectives of case study

❑ To give practical experience of investigation, analysis and design, reporting and presentation to participants

❏ To demonstrate the need for methodology in Systems Engineering

❏ To demonstrate the need to set goals and milestones

❏ To demonstrate the need for communication between individuals

❏ To emphasise the human relationship aspect of any SEM.

Summary of Rent and Charge Collection Timings

❏ Community Charge is normally paid in April and October of a particular year.

❏ Rents are paid weekly by Thursday of the current week number, by arrangement, or by direct payment methods. On public holidays – every fortnight.

❏ Reminders: *First written reminder from district or head office supervisor.*
Second reminder after 10 working days from letter one.
Third warning of possible legal action after 20 working days from letter two, sent by the district officers.

❏ Rent reports for head office done by the month end.

❏ Charge reports done by the month after the due dates.

❏ New tenants, empty properties and arrears/non payments of rents are reported with returns to head office.

❏ The head office timetable is exactly the same as the district office's, but the deputy housing officer collates all reports and meets with the housing manager on Tuesday after the rent collection to discuss any problems. There are also meetings with the housing and charge sub committees of the council every month, at which reports, problems and progress are discussed. These are normally held on the last Friday morning of the month in the civic hall.

❏ *Ad-hoc* enquiries by the public take 10 working days to resolve, and those by other council staff take three working days.

See Appendix II operational timetable for an overview

Case Study

Suggested Outline Solution

Management Specification

Contents

Section

1. Introduction

1.1 Purpose of the Specification

The purpose of this specification is to provide a basis for a decision to be made by the management of the Departments of Housing and Finance as to whether this specification fulfils the requirements of a Rent and Community Charge Accounting System. It is produced as a sequel to *A Feasibility Study into the data Processing Requirements of the Department of Housing for a full Housing Rent Accounting System*, produced in December 1989 and subsequently approved by the Computer Sub-Committee.

1.2 Terms of Reference

❑ The original terms of reference for the feasibility study are attached as Appendix 1.

❑ To work within the costs agreed in the Feasibility Report for:
>   User departments
>   Systems and programming development
>   Computer hardware and operating.
>   Report any variations to these costs.

❑ To work within the implementation timetable agreed in the Feasibility Study, or report any variations.

1.3 Method of Work

No detailed examination of equipment has been included in this specification. But a brief examination of the systems available for cash reciepting, networking and communication with the central system leads us to believe that no serious problems will be met in this area. We do recommend that proper tender documents should be written, and tenders from suppliers sought on the basis of our design. The Terms of Reference were discussed in some detail with senior management of the Department of Housing and subsequently with the staff of that department. An outline system was devised and agreed in principle.

Visits were made to Barford MDC (part GIRO) and Newcastle-upon-Clyde (office payment only) to examine their respective computer systems and the findings proved useful and were duly noted.

The findings of the Department of Housing were analysed together with the requirements of the department of Administration and Computer Services Division, and the Department of Finance – Budgets and Audit Division, as the basis for the design of the Rent Accounting System, as well as the old centralised rent and charge rates system.

2. System Description

2.1 Design Aims

The system is designed with the following aims:

❏ To adhere to the terms of reference.

❏ To supersede the existing Rents and Rates system.

❏ To provide a basis for comprehensive management information.

❏ To allow flexibility for future system enhancements.

❏ To link to the proposed Housing Rebates system.

❏ To link into the new leisure and recreation payment, ticketing and booking system.

2.2 System Functions

The functions of the system are:

❏ To create and maintain a tenant's data containing a history of transactions for each account record.

❏ To create and maintain a housing property master file holding data for each property.

❏ To post rents and community charge payments received, input by various methods to the tenant's master file but allow standing orders, deductions from salaries/wages and direct DSS payments regardless of the method of cash collection chosen.

❏ A facility to update the master file via terminals.

❏ Preparation of rent cards at the beginning of each financial year.

❏ Automatic raising of tenant notifications for rent and community charge changes.

❏ Management information to enable improved control to be maintained on void properties.

❏ Analysis of income.

❏ Facility to interrogate the database via terminals plus the facility to enable Housing Management to produce their own *ad-hoc* reports.

❏ Automatic monitoring of arrears.

❏ To allow rent increase/decrease calculations based on pre-defined criteria.

❏ By holding the UPRN, provide a link to the Council's database. This will be transferred from the existing Housing Rents System.

❏ Produce weekly DP strips until outside collection is terminated, half the file being printed on alternate weeks.

An outline management specification for computer runs for each department appears in Appendix I.

2.3 Procedure Used

Data storage

❏ Details of all the tenants will be maintained on a disc- based master file.

❏ Details of all properties will be maintained on a separate disc-based master file.

❏ Details of all charge payers will be maintained on a disc-based master file.

❏ The reference number used by the system is eight characters in length and would be present on both master files.

❏ Characters 3 to 6 will be a sequential property number within that estate office.

❏ Character 7 will be a check digit with a value of 0 to 9 or X, determined by a modulus 11 calculation.

Daily Interrogations

The central computer files containing tenant property and chargedetailswill be available for interrogation throughout the day. Access will be via terminals at various locations specified by the Housing Department. The basis for interrogations will be either the property reference number or property address (the latter will generate the reference number automatically using UGEN). As payments, voids and arrears form the basis of the system, all three are dealt with individually later. However, to clarify their use they are introduced in their appropriate sections following.

Daily Run

The purpose of the daily run is to:

❏ Update the tenants master file with payment received from the various methods of input.

❏ Accumulate tenancy changes for a weekly update.

❏ Produce a daily payment receipts summary for reconciliation with payments due.

Weekly Run

The purpose of the weekly run is to:

❏ Update the property master file with new tenants, amendments and so on (having been accepted and stored during the week) giving an update listing, then transfer the calculated weekly debit to the tenants master file.

❏ Produce the weekly rental print, split between family dwellings and miscellaneous properties.

❏ Produce the summary of weekly rental, split between dwellings and miscellaneous properties.

❏ Link to the existing housing rebates system.

❏ Produce the present void property listing and weekly analysis of voids.

❏ Produce arrears information as required.

❏ Produce the weekly cash receipts summary (showing total for the week).

❏ Produce listings of terminations where arrears/credits not outstanding.

Monthly Run

There will be no specific monthly run unless required for the CC system.

Quarterly Run

The purpose of the quarterly run is to:

❏ Produce totals of accumulative debit to date.

❏ Print accumulative figures from daily cash receipts.

❏ Produce final rental summary.

Half-yearly Runs

The purpose of the half-yearly run is to:

❏ Zero the accumulative totals on the property master file.

❑ Bring forward the year-end balance, if any, on each tenant's record.

❑ Microfiche the tenants file and delete the last but one half-yearly details – move the details remaining down the tenant's record.

❑ Delete old terminated tenancy records from the tenants master file where the balance is zero.

❑ Delete property records taken out of charge at end of year.

❑ Produce rent cards for all tenants containing new year's community charge and rents.

❑ Similarly for CC register.

Run as Required

Various reports will be produced by the submission of appropriate documentation to the Computer Services Division.

Examples of the reports which should be available are:

❑ Batch interrogation of the property master file by individual reference, range of references or overall for reports.

❑ Batch interrogation of the tenant master file by individual reference, range of references or overall for reports.

❑ *Ad-hoc* reports based on arrears and void details held on the master files at off-peak times.

2.4 Controls

Comprehensive controls will be maintained by the system for both the computer master files and for data entry.

Property Master Records

Control records will be maintained both at area level and overall file level. These will be checked by the Housing Department on each weekly update and any discrepancies notified to Computer Services – Control Section for investigation.

Tenant Master Records

Control records will be maintained both at estate level and overall level and overall file total. These will be updated daily by the appropriate values and checked by the Housing Department on each weekly update and any discrepancies notified to the Computer Services – Control Section for investigation.

Data Entry Controls

Data will be input directly by Housing staff. The computer will maintain throughout the day, counts of the number of documents and transactions entered. These totals will be printed at the end of the day for checking by the Housing Department.

General Controls

Each master file update will result in control records being printed for numbers of arrears letters and son on produced. These controls will be reconciled by the Housing Department against actual numbers printed, as indicated by the print program.

File Security

Two magnetic tape security copies of the previous weekly update master files will be produced automatically and retained with the appropriate input data files. Two copies will be taken during the day, of transactions accepted through the video terminals.

Security of File Access

Passwords at appropriate levels will ensure security of access to the property and tenant master files via the terminals at the area offices.

Similarly, passwords will ensure that unauthorised personnel are not able to input information for subsequent use during the file updating procedures.

These passwords can be changed at any time by the Housing Department.

2.5 Void Procedures

The documenting of information which affects voids can be split into three procedures.

Property Becoming Empty

❏ The estate office will enter the reference number and tenancy termination date through the video terminal.

❏ Providing the termination date is for the week being processed, the record will be held in the computer ready for the weekly update.

❏ If the termination is for a week prior to the week being processed, information will be passed to the video terminal/printer at Head Office to allow retrospective void financial details to be manually calculated and entered to the computer. The record will still be held in the computer for the weekly update.

Empty Property Re-let

❑ The estate office will enter the new reference number, new tenant's name and tenancy commencement date through the video terminal using the check digit calculation chart.

❑ The computer will check the reference number (tenant's sequence number and check digit) and the record will be held in the computer ready for the weekly update.

Property becoming empty and re-let same week

Procedure exactly the same as for above.

All amendments to the file will be proof listed and checked by the Housing Department.

A weekly voids file will be created ready for sorting into chronological order within estate offices. A weekly listing identifying each void record, showing reference number, property type, reason for void, date of termination, number of times offered and so on, will be produced. The Housing Department will examine each entry of a void property, and where the reason for void changes from that previously stated, an input overwriting the existing reason is needed.

A weekly analysis of numbers of void properties by estate office, i.e. property type and length of void period (in bands) will be produced.

A quarterly analysis of void periods will be output, analysing lettings during the quarter for each estate office, showing length of void period (in bands) for each property type, aggregates for the year and average void periods for types of property within estate offices.

2.6 Arrears Control

The tenancy is weekly and rent is therefore due each week. Where outside collections are carried out, they will be on a fortnightly basis. Tenants may, therefore, pay either weekly or fortnightly in arrears. Tenants paying fortnightly wil lbe able to pay on whichever of the two weeks they choose. Where tenants pay monthly in arrears, no action wil lbe taken where regular payments are made in full within the month.

The computer will be used to perform as many of the routine tasks associated with arrears control as possible, e.g. production of letters, weekly monitoring of Notice to Quit cases. This will enable the Housing Assistants to spend less time on these tasks, and more time making contact with tenants in arrears at the earliest possible stage.

Arrears Letters (not garages – see later)

There will be three arrears letters:

(I) Mild reminder

(II) Stronger reminder

(III) Follow-up letter to (I) and (II).

❑ Arrears letter (I). To be sent under the following circumstances:

> Balance is 3 x weekly debit or more, but less than 4 x weekly debit, except where:
>
> (i) Arrears letter (I) has been sent within last 13 weeks, or
>
> (ii) Payment type indicator shows DSS, Bankers Order, Giro, Salary/Wages deduction, Monthly payer, Committee tenancies, suspend arrears procedure, or
>
> (iii) Current balance exceeds last week's balance plus 1 x weekly debit, or
>
> (iv) Current balance is less than previous week's balance.

If (i) above applies, an arrears letter (II) shall be produced subject to (ii), (iii) and (iv).

❑ Arrears letter (III). To be sent under the following circumstances:

> Balance is 4 x weekly debit or more, but less than 5 x weekly debit, except where (ii), (iii) and (iv) above apply.

Arrears Balances of Five Week's Rent and More

When a debt reaches five weeks or more, a visit to the home must be made. At this stage the computer will indicate, by report, that a visit is required and will repeat such indication each subsequent week until either the visit is made followed by the appropriate input, or the debt reduces to less than five weeks. A visit form will be printed by the computer for each case indicated.

Service of Notice

If the debt continues to increase, the case should be submitted for approval to serve notice when the debt reaches weekly debit x 7 unless submitted earlier. At this stage, the computer will report all appropriate cases and continue to do so until the Notice Indicator is cancelled by an input signifying that notice has been served on the tenant.

A form H/C 108 (submission for approval) will be produced at the time of the first indication of notice being necessary. Shortly before the notice lapses, after 12 months, the computer will print a report indicating the need for a fresh notice.

After notice has been served, the computer will show the current balance against the balance at the time of service, and subsequently against the balance at the time of expiry. (See *Weekly Report*).

Court Action

There will be provision to hold on file the date of any Court Hearing for Possession and this information will appear on reports.

Arrangements

There will be provision to hold details of arrangements made with tenants for reducing arrears levels by payment of fixed weekly amounts. The same field should be used to record details of suspended possession orders.

Weekly Report

A weekly report will be produced by collection code (by collector), showing the following information for every tenancy where either arrears are 3 x weekly debit or more, or a debit balance of less than 3 x weekly debit has existed for the past three weeks.

Reference number
Name
Address
Weekly charge
Last week's balance
This week's balance
Account adjustment
Letters produced this week
Visits required/form produced
Notice required/served
Arrears at service/expire of notice
Date of court hearing
Arrangement amount

This report will list all cases in order of category thus:

Debts of less than three weeks
Debts where letters produced
Debts requiring visit
Debts requiring notice
Debts of more than seven weeks

Cases will be listed in ascending order of size of debt within each category.

Monitoring of Arrears by Housing Manager/Area Manager

The weekly report outlined above is produced for initial action by the Housing Assistant, who will make a note against each code on the report to indicate the action taken where appropriate. This report will be examined by the Housing Manager and will form the basis of the Area Manager's monitoring.

Statistical Information

Analysis of the arrears will show bandings of the arrears by cash amounts and multiples of weekly debit for each area, estate office and collection code. Further analysis will show the arrears in respect of DSS, monthly payment, N/Q cases, court cases and so on.

Computer Arrears System for Garage Tenancies

❑ Arrears Letter (I) to be generated where:

> Account balance is 6 x weekly debit or more, but less than 8 x weekly debit, except:

> (i) where Arrears Letter (I) has been sent within the last 13 weeks, in which case substitute Arrears Letter (II), or

> (ii) payment type indicator shows DSS, Banker's Order, Giro etc., or

> (iii) current balance exceeds last week's balance plus 1 x weekly debit, or

> (iv) current balance balance is less than previous week's balance.

❑ Arrears Letter (II) to be generated where:-

> Account balance is 8 x weekly or more, but less than 9 x debit, except for circumstances in (i), (iii) or (iv) above.

> Link with letter produced for dwelling tenancy arrears.

The operational timetable is contained in Appendix II.

4. Data Files and Volumes

4.1 Master Files

Property Records

Number of records	10,000
Average number of characters on file	29 million
Number of little links	23,000
Growth rate	negligible

Tenant Records

Number of records	110,000
Average number of characters on file	244 million
Number of little links	225,000
Growth rate	10% during the year

4.2 Output Files

Daily Runs

Number of lines of print   60 lines
(All the daily output will be printed at the civic hall.)

Weekly Runs

Number of lines of print   67,500 lines
(Including DP strips)
(All weekly output will be printed at the civic hall.)

Quarterly Runs

Number of lines of print.   10,000 lines

(All quarterly output will be printed at the civic hall.)

Annual Runs

Rent cards   350,000 lines

4.3 Database Contents

The key to the records on the property and tenant files is seven characters in length and is determined as follows:

Characters 1 and 2   Estate office number in the range 01 to 40.

Characters 3 to 6   Sequential property number with the estate office.

Character 7   Sequential number of the latest tenant in that property.

An eighth digit makes up the full reference number and is a modulus 11 check digit.

The files will be maintained in ascending key sequence.

Property File requirements

The file will consist of records of the following type and in the following sequence:

❏ Property records within an estate office

❏ Estate office control record

❏ Overall file control record.

Property records

These records consist of the following data fields:

❏ UPRN – unique property reference number

❏ Reference – in form as previously described

❏ Tenant's name

❏ Tenancy commenced date – date on which the tenancy commenced.

❏ Type of property.

❏ Estate number – to which the property relates.

❏ CC reference number – to allow the link to the council's CC system.

❏ Gross value – gross value of the property.

❏ Collector number – number allocated to each collector at an estate office.

❏ Water code – water code applicable to the property.

❑ Normal net rent – when the normal net rent is non-standard.

❑ Water – indicates the weekly value of water to be paid on the property.

❑ General service charge – the weekly value of general service charge to be paid.

❑ Central heating – amount payable in respect of central heating charges.

❑ Fiveadditional charges – amounts payable under the various additional charge code.

❑ Total gross rent – addition of the previous six fields

❑ Rent rebates – input to this system from the present Rebate system.

❑ Weekly charge – total gross rent minus the rent and CC rebate.

❑ Accumulatives – accumulatives of the above financial fields.

❑ Uncodeable address – present when the UPRN generated address is not felt to be a ·quate for housing needs.

❑ ge cross-reference – to link a tenant to a garage and vice versa.

F 'fice control records

These ٺ. ٺist of the following data fields:

❑ Reference – estate number followed by 9s.

❑ Number of property records in that estate office.

❑ Accumulative CC value for the estate office.

❑ Total weekly charge for that estate office.

Overall control records

This record has exactly the same format as the Estate Office Control Record – the totals held being for the whole file.

Tentant File requirements

The file will consist of records of the following type and in the following sequence:

❑ Tenant's details within an estate office.

❑ Suspense accounts within an estate office.

❑ Estate office control record.

❑ Overall file control record.

Estate Office tenant details

These records consist of the following data fields:

❑ Reference – in form as previously described.

❑ Tenant's name.

❑ Weeknumberof start of tenancy – during current year.

❑ Method of payment – indicates the method of payment chosen by the tenant – if deducted from salary or wage a man number will also be held.

❑ Credit status – tenant's credit status.

❑ Start of year balance – balance on the tenant's account at the start of the financial year.

❑ Current balance – Present balance on the tenant's account.

❑ Tenancy termination date – date on which tenancy terminated.

❑ Weekly details – details of the weekly debt, transactions (date, type, till number and amount) and balance from start of year or start of tenancy.

❑ Arrears notice dates – dates on which notices were produced.

❑ Garage indicator – signifies tenant also has a garage account.

Suspense account records

These   will contain a balance and payment and/or adjustment details to enable incorrect payments to be adjusted manually.

Estate office control records

These consist of the following data fields:

❑ Reference – in form as previously described.

❑ Start of year balance – the accumulated balance at the start of the year for that estate office.

❑ Current balance – the accumulated balance at the current time for that estate office.

❏ Weekly charge – accumulated weekly charge for that estate office for that week.

❏ Transaction code details – accumulative figures for each transaction.

Overall control record

This record has exactly the same format as the Estate Office Control Record – the totals being for the whole file.

Community Charge requirements

These records consist of the following data fields:

❏ UCCRN – unique community charge reference number.

❏ Payer's name – the charge payer's name.

❏ Commencement date – date at which the payer entered the system.

❏ Transfer date – date at which the payer left the system.

❏ UPRN – unique property reference number to link in with the council's rent system.

❏ Address details – the full postal address of the property.

❏ Charge type – i.e. domestic or business.

❏ Gross payment amount – the amount of charge payed.

❏ Payment type – i.e. weekly, wages/salary deduction, monthly, etc.

❏ Payment amounts – the amount payed each time.

Arrears details will be handled the same way as rent arrears, but will have to take into account that it is usual for the demand to be in 10 monthly amounts, and to be paid either in full, in halves, quarters, or monthly.

Costs and Resources

6.1 Equipment

The following is a unit cost per office:

	COST	ANNUAL MAINTENANCE
	£	£
1 x cash reciepting machine	2,522	264
2 x video terminals	3,900	484
1 x printer	800	168
2 x page printing adapter.	700	-
1 x M.I.U.	765	108
2 x cable	90	-
1 x modem	475	-
1 x microfiche viewer	150	–
	£9,402	£1,024

plus GPO charges (lines, installation fee).

Civic Hall equipment

1 modem per estate office – £475 each

1 card per terminal £250 plus £6 maintenance per year.

Disc drives and ancillary equipment for data to and from estate offices as required – £300 - £400

6.2 Development Costs

	£
Systems (35 man weeks)	18,375
Programming (63 man weeks) (18 programs + 8 TPRs)	26,460
Computer time (210 tests)	10,500
Amendments to payroll system	4,000
Amendments to rebate system	1,500
File creation: S – 5.5 weeks, P – 7 weeks, C – 12 tests	6,427
	£67,262
10% for contingencies	6,726
	£73,988

6.3 Operating Costs

An accurate figure is impossible to access for this system. However, costs have been based on similar smaller systems.

Running cost for the year excluding maintenance of equipment: £250,000

7. Benefits of the System

❏ Speedier and more efficient balancing of the rent accounts, leaving more staff time for housing management duties.

❏ Provides a greater control over the rent accounting system for the Finance Section at Head Office.

❏ Provides a comprehensive alternative to outside collection when a complete or partial withdrawal of that facility occurs in the future.

❏ Provides better arrears control.

❏ Provides better void property control.

❏ Provides management with comprehensive details of estate office performance if required.

❏ Allows for better arrangements from staffing point of view, e.g. holidays.

❏ Provides immediate access to tenant's accounts with the provision of up-to-date arrears position etc.

❏ The provision of better control over Banker's Order payments with tenants being advised of new monthly payments at the beginning of the financial year and when rent changes occur.

❏ Direct input of weekly returns, tenancy terminations and re-lets,therebysavingtimespentondocumentation atHead Office.

❏ Identification of DSS direct payments will lead to benefits on termination of tenancy and transfer cases.

❏ Provides for an alternative, (e.g. Monday to Friday) to the present rent week, which is of benefit to both the tenant and the department.

❏ Reduce the amount of DP Strip stationary required as only half the amount printed each week until phased out.

8. Suggested context DFD for Barchester system

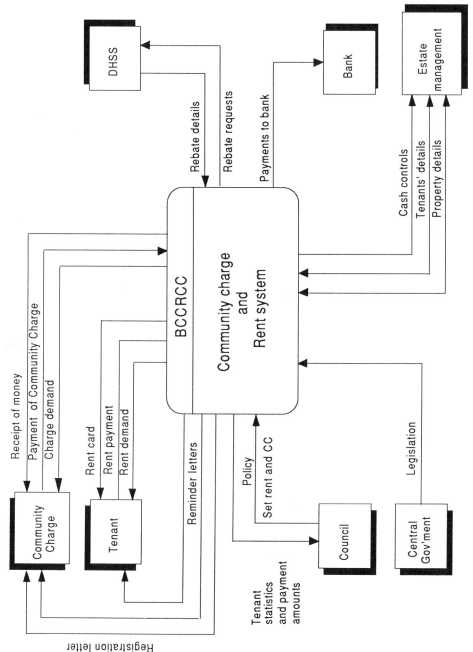

Suggested Level 1 DFD

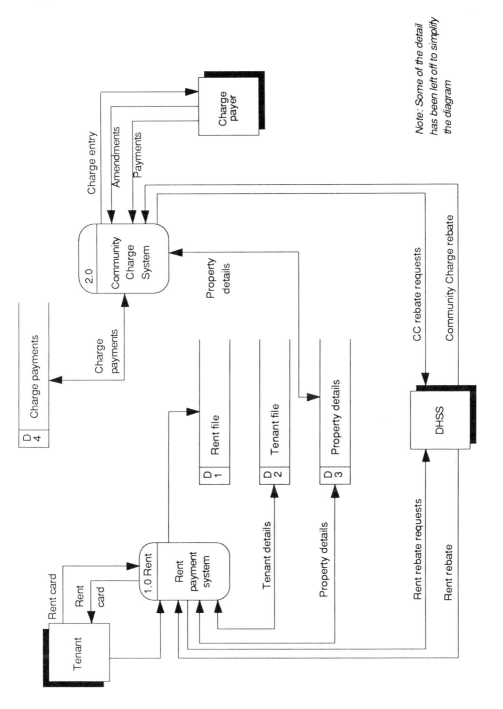

Note: Some of the detail has been left off to simplify the diagram

Suggested Level 2 DFD logical for rent payments

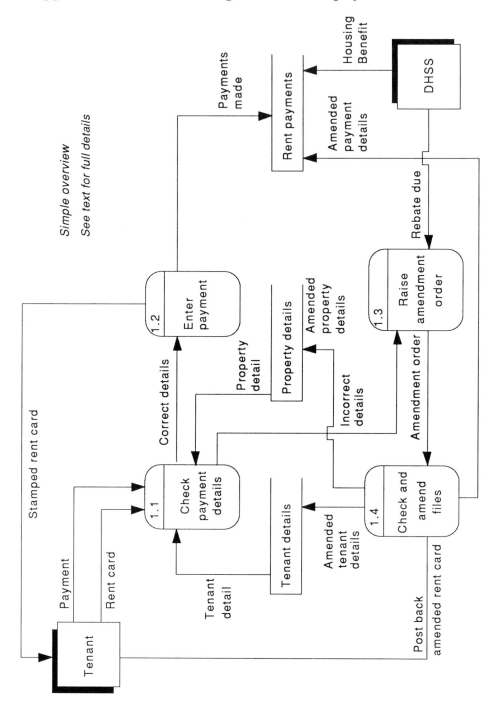

9. Implementation Timetable

Event \ Date	June	July	Aug	Sept	Oct	Nov	Dec	Jan	Feb	Mar	Apr
Produce and circulate specification	▓										
Presentation and approval		▓									
Ordering of computer terminal equipment		▓	▓								
Order GPO lines						▓					
Preparation of program specification			▓	▓							
Program writing and testing					▓	▓	▓	▓			
Preparation of user manual						▓	▓	▓			
Order special stationery								▓			
System/user testing									▓		
Staff training										▓	▓
File creation									▓	▓	▓
Delivery of computer equipment										▓	▓
Parallel running										▓	
Phased implementation											▓

10. Samples of Inputs and Outputs

Screen Inputs/Outputs

❏ New property and initial tenancy or standard detail amendments (opposite).

❏ Additional charges.

❏ CC and rent rebate amendments (page 177).

❏ Accumulative amendments (page 178).

❏ Cash entered response (terminal) plus receipt at till and stamped rent card (Figures 9.1, 9.4 and page 179). The mechanism for issue of cash receipts and stamping the rent card is shown in Appendix II.

❏ Full history of tenant's record – terminal (opposite and pages 177, 178).

❏ Output reports required.

❏ Summary of daily cash receipts.

❏ Property file proof list and full file print.

❏ Tenant's file full file print.

❏ Weekly rentals.

❏ Summary of weekly rentals.

❏ Weekly void property listing.

❏ Weekly analysis of voids.

❏ Weekly terminations with outstanding arrears/credits.

❏ Weekly statement of arrears by collector.

❏ Weekly statement of arrears by estate office.

❏ Weekly estate office arrears in bands of weeks.

❏ Quarterly accumulative final rental summary.

❏ Quarterly accumulative daily cash receipts.

❏ Quarterly totals of accumulative debit to date.

VDU DISPLAY WORKSHEET

PROJECT: BCC RCC

VERSION: 1.0 SECTION: 1.0
DATE: 03/03/90 PAGE: 31A

Tenancy Rool

Reference
CC Ref

Property Details:
Type Value
No

Name

Rent
ABR
CC Code
CC Amnt
CC Var

Commenced Date :

General Service Charges IF applicable

Water Code Water Variation
Service Service Var

Disablement
Relief Val Relief Amnt

Address
Postcode

TENANCY MAINTENANCE

Additional charges
Code
Ref
Var
Amt

Date :

[DDMMYY]

Add Change Search Forward Back Delete Recover List Exit Help

VDU DISPLAY WORKSHEET

PROJECT: Bcc Rcc

VERSION: 1·0   SECTION: 10

DATE: Ø3/Ø3/9Ø   PAGE: 31B

```
Rebate RØØ2          REBATE AMEND              Date :

Rent Details              Community Charge

  Ref [   ]   Rent [ . ]         Ref [   ]    cc  [ . ]
              Var  [ . ]                      Var [ . ]

Accumulative Amendments []




[Search] [Add] [Exit] [Help]
```

Accumulative amendments displayed on screen.

VDU DISPLAY WORKSHEET | PROJECT: Bcc Rcc | VERSION: 1·0 | SECTION: 10 | DATE: 03/03/90 | PAGE: 31C

ACCUMULATIVE AMENDMENTS

New

Previous

Rebate2 Ro03

Ref

G·S·C
N·N·R
C·d
WATER
C·H
DISABLE
CHARGE

1
2
3

T·G·R
Rent Rebate
CC Rebate
Weekly Charge
N·N·R (Voids)
CC (Voids)
Water (Voids)
GSC (Voids)

Search   List   Exit   Help

VDU DISPLAY WORKSHEET	PROJECT: Bcc Rcc	VERSION: 1.0 SECTION: 1.0 DATE: 03/03/90 PAGE: 31D

Cash   Date ::

Tenancy   [X]   Name   [A]   CASH ENTERED

Ref   [X]   [A]

Weekly Charge [999.99]   Amount Entered [999.99]   Date Entered [DDMMYY]

Balance Outstanding   [999.99]   Date For

After Payment   [999.99]

[Add] [Search] [Delete] [Recovered] [List] [Exit] [Help]

Date for is the week ending date for the payment

11. The Effect on Other Systems

The system has been designed to link into the Council's existing Housing Rebates system. The only change required to the present system is to reference all the existing cases.

As addresses will not be held in the system, thorough the UPRN, addresses will be automatically generated using the Council's database.

Although the present payroll system will accept information input for new andamended debits to allow deductionsfrom salary/wages, it is felt desirable that significant changes should be made to accommodate the full requirements of both systems. Consideration has been given to the transfer of detailsforemployees leaving Councilproperties and tenants becoming Council employees. Information about deductions will be passed to Payroll as weekly amounts with any variations documented manually. Exact details of responsibilities still have tobe determined.

12. Future Developments

A link to the existing lapsed Tenancy system although possible, was not, at this time, felt desirable.

Accounts for tenants terminating properties when arrears are outstanding could be raised automatically, however, it was felt a long period of consolidation following implementation should take place before such a link was made.

Link into payment for council owned leisure facilities such as badminton courts, or theatres may be possible.

Appendix I

Terms of Reference for a Feasibility Study

1. The Computer Sub-Committee, on 17th July 1989 considered departmental priorities for computer development, and instructed a feasibility study to be prepared into a Housing Rents System.

2. The report should cover the data processing requirements for a full Housing Rent Accounting system, and should be completed by 30th November 1989.

3. The proposed system should cater for all aspects of Rent Accounting, and should carry out functions under the following broad headings:

❑ Rent collection

❑ Arrears collection

❑ Rent and CC Rebates

3.1 Rent collection

(a) The calculation of the weekly charge for each property.

(b) To produce rent card/payment vouchers for each property at the beginning of the financial year.

(c) To re-calculate the rent/CC upon a rent/CC increase or decreaseand to provide for the rent change tobe applied by several different methods.

(d) To prepare a rent change notice for each tenancy prior to the change being applied, and to provide DSS with such relevant information.

(e) To provide for the speedy input of cash payment information, and to allow payment to be made by several different methods, i.e. cash, Giro, office collection, outside collection, standing order, deduction from wages/salary etc.

(f) The efficient and accurate maintenance of tenants' accounts.

(g) Production of information to permit the more efficient collection of rent arrears and lapsed tenancy debts.

(h) Provision of the fullest information regarding those transactions affecting a tenant's account.

(i) Provision of proper accounting controls over all transactions.

(j) Provision of statistical information for management.

(k) Notification of changes to debit and follow-up procedures.

(l) Ability to provide tenants with statements of accounts.

3.2 Arrears collection

(a) Ability to determine the priority for the collection of arrears.

(b) Efficient administration of arrears follow-up procedures.

(c) Reduction of arrears.

(d) Arrangement facilities.

(e) Provide meaningful controls of arrears by districts.

3.3 Rent and CC Rebates

(a) To provide an efficient and effective administration of the rent and CC rebate granting process.

(b) Provide an automatic interface to rent collection procedures.

(c) Provide CC rebate information to CC Department.

(d) Provide information regarding tenants.

(e) Provide up-to-date and accurate information regarding rebate applications to tenants and to the Housing Department.

4. Systems of other Local Authorities may be examined to determine if any may be of use as the basis for a system.

5. The main processing will be carried out on the Council's proposed computer system, but it will be necessary to consider the use of cash reciepting and terminal equipment at various locations.

6. The study should take into account as far as possible the tasks currently being undertaken by the Policy Unit:

(a) The review of the Departmental structures with regard to the Housing Department.

(b) Any further decentralisation of the Housing function.

7. The report should include:

(a) An outline of the proposed system.

(b) The costs and benefits of the proposals.

(c) The timescale for the implementation.

(d) Alternatives considered and the reason for rejection.

The report will be written jointly by the Housing Department and the Computer Services Division.

Appendix II: Supporting Documents

Operational Timetable

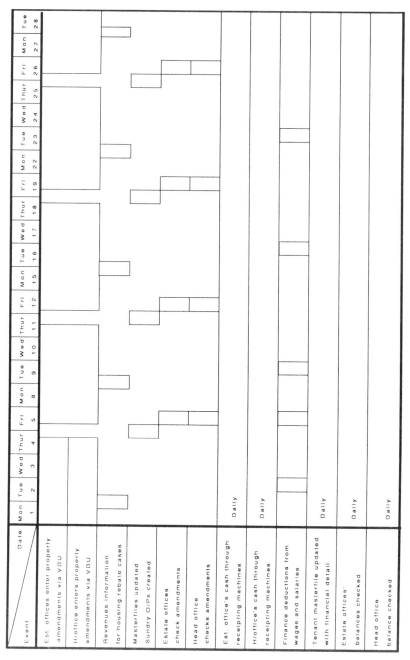

System flowchart into Departmental Management Specification

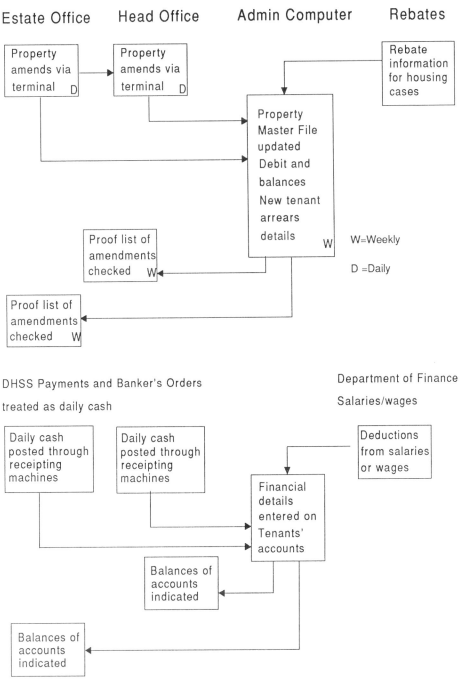

Cash Receipting Procedures

Rent card provided   No rent card provided

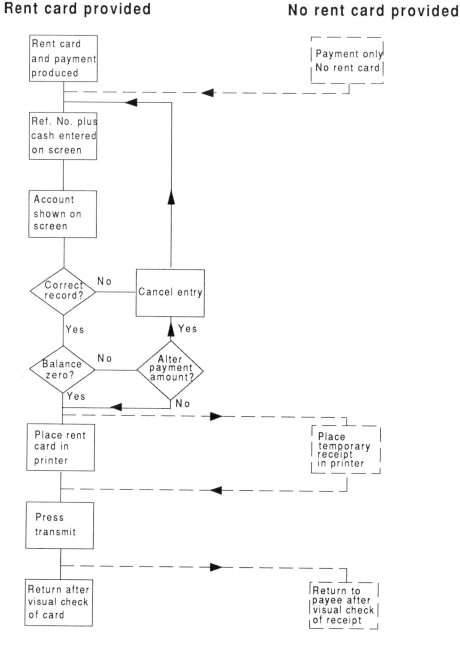

*Collector's cash will be input via the VDU (back office)
entering reference number and value*

Appendix III: Old System Runchart

Daily run (A)

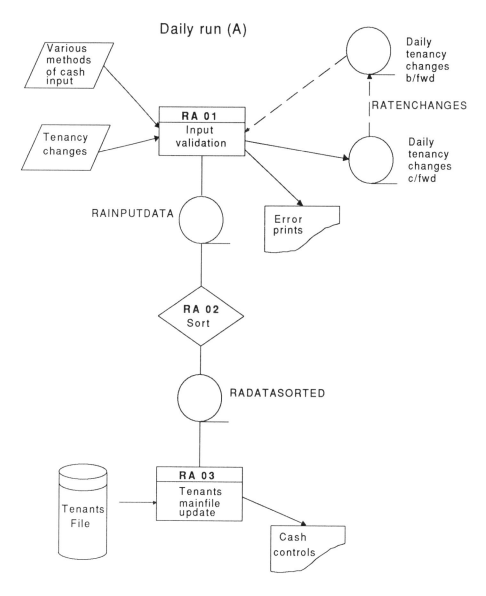

Daily run (A)

Various methods of cash input

Tenancy changes

RA 01
Input validation

Daily tenancy changes b/fwd

RATENCHANGES

Daily tenancy changes c/fwd

Error prints

RAINPUTDATA

RA 02
Sort

RADATASORTED

Tenants File

RA 03
Tenants mainfile update

Cash controls

Daily run (B)

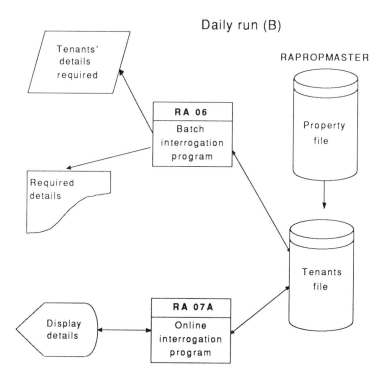

Daily run (B)

Also as part of the weekly run

Weekly run

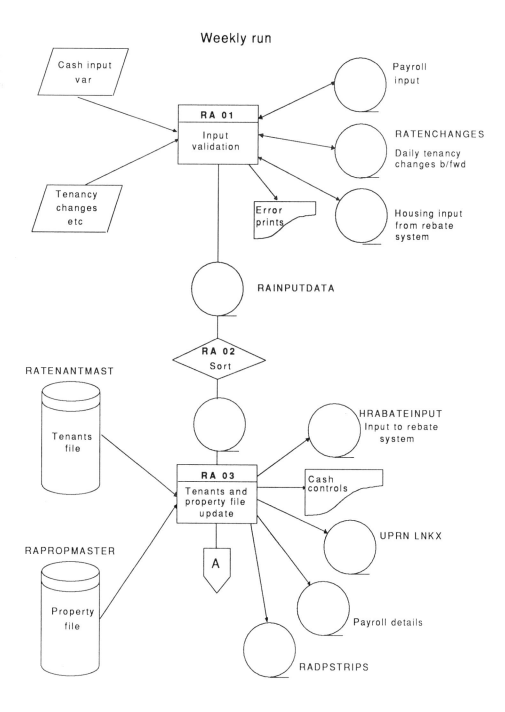

Weekly run

Weekly run (continued)

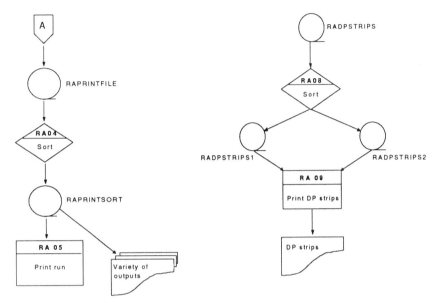

Runs as required

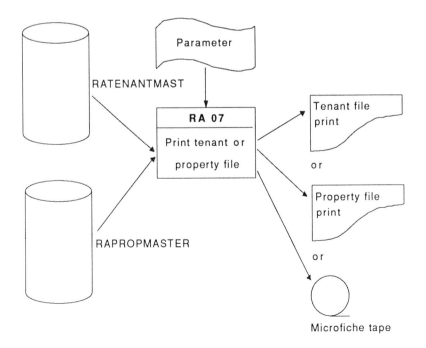

Year end

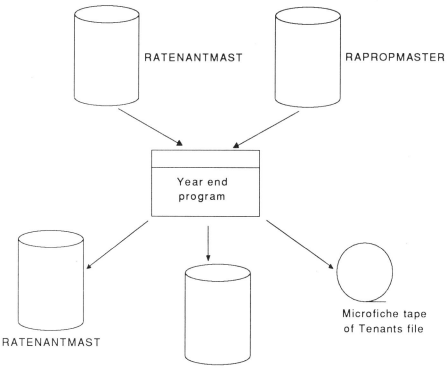

Jobs to do at the year end:

1) Zero weeks 1-26 on Tenants file and move other details down

2) Drop old records on Tenants file when account = zero

3) Carry forward start of year balances

4) Drop accumulators on property file

Rent card

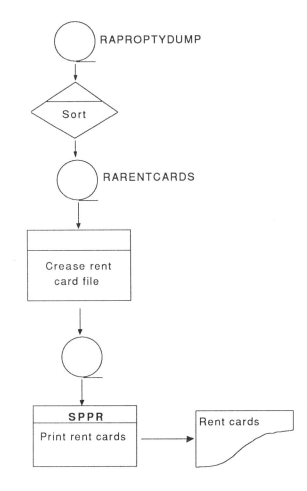

Security dump/Reset

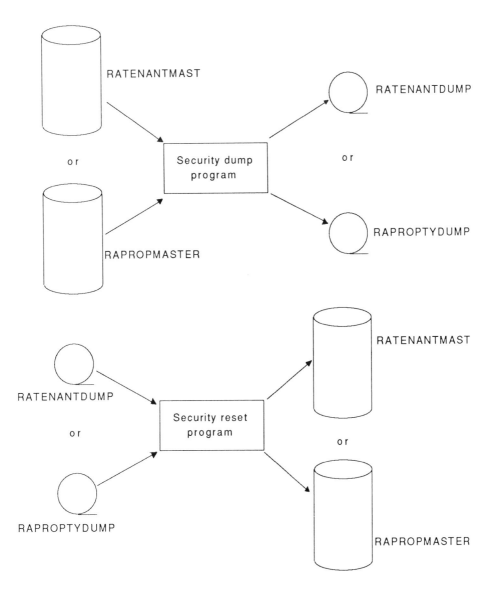

Rent calculation

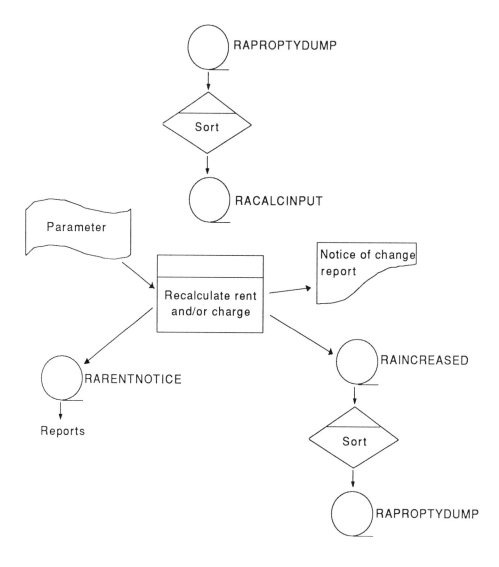

Rent calculation (continued)

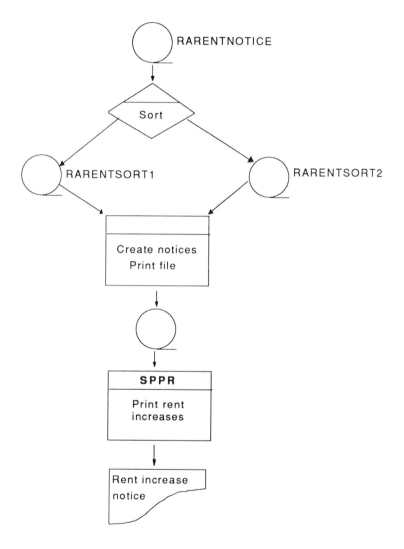

INDEX